KT-212-654

e-mail@work

get moving with digital
communication

Jonathan Whelan

technology is everybody's business

PEARSON EDUCATION LIMITED

Head Office:
Edinburgh Gate
Harlow CM20 2JE
Tel: +44 (0)1279 623623
Fax: +44 (0)1279 431059

London Office:
128 Long Acre
London WC2E 9AN
Tel: +44 (0)20 7447 2000
Fax: +44 (0)20 7240 5771
Website: www.business-minds.com

KING ALFRED'S COLLEGE
WINCHESTER

02466284 | 004·692
WHE

First published in Great Britain in 2000

© Jonathan Whelan 2000

The right of Jonathan Whelan to be identified as Author
of this Work has been asserted by him in accordance
with the Copyright, Designs and Patents Act 1988.

ISBN 0 273 64465 3

British Library Cataloguing in Publication Data
A CIP catalogue record for this book can be obtained from the British Library

All rights reserved; no part of this publication may be reproduced, stored
in a retrieval system, or transmitted in any form or by any means, electronic,
mechanical, photocopying, recording, or otherwise without either the prior
written permission of the Publishers or a licence permitting restricted copying
in the United Kingdom issued by the Copyright Licensing Agency Ltd,
90 Tottenham Court Road, London W1P 0LP. This book may not be lent,
resold, hired out or otherwise disposed of by way of trade in any form
of binding or cover other than that in which it is published, without the
prior consent of the Publishers.

This publication is designed to provide accurate and authoritative information
in regard to the subject matter covered. It is sold with the understanding that
neither the author nor the publisher is engaged in rendering legal, investing,
or any other professional service. If legal advice or other expert assistance is
required, the service of a competent professional person should be sought.

The author, publisher and contributors make no representations, express or
implied, with regard to the accuracy or completeness of the information
contained in this book and cannot accept any responsibility or liability for
any loss or damage arising from any information, instructions, advice, errors
or omissions that it may contain.

10 9 8 7 6 5 4 3

Typeset by Northern Phototypesetting Co. Ltd, Bolton
Printed and bound in Great Britain by Biddles Ltd, Guildford and King's Lynn

The Publishers' policy is to use paper manufactured from sustainable forests.

about the author

Jonathan Whelan graduated from the University of Wales, Aberystwyth, with an honours degree in mathematics. He then trained as a teacher and, following a period of teaching secondary school mathematics, in 1986 he entered the field of information technology.

Since then Jonathan has performed many varied roles ranging from computer system design to project and quality management. As well as having considerable practical experience he is also a chartered engineer, a member of the British Computer Society and a member of the Institute of Quality Assurance.

In recent years, as a business systems consultant, he has focused on the significance of technology to businesses and in particular the opportunities and issues that face business users of technology.

When not consulting, Jonathan writes on business technology issues. A broad spectrum of businesses have benefited from his observations and a number of his papers have led to significant programmes of work within corporate organizations.

In 1997 Jonathan's first book was published, titled *The Year 2000 Computer Problem: A practical guide for businesses*. It was an extremely successful publication and attracted acclaim from government, business and professional organizations.

If you have any comments about this book, you can contact Jonathan at his e-mail address: author@jonathanwhelan.com

To Lindsay and Lizzie
For the love, the patience, the smiles

contents

foreword ● x
Steve Ballmer, President and CEO, Microsoft Corporation

acknowledgments ● xii

preface ● xiv

1 introduction

the communications revolution ● 2

effect of e-mail in business ● 6

e-mail as a business risk ● 11

making e-mail work for you ● 15

e-mail in practice ● 20

summary ● 23

2 a closer look at e-mail

e-mail's key characteristics ● 26

e-mail and related topics ● 34

the future of e-mail ● 43

summary ● 48

3 managing your mail

why manage your mail? ● 50

managing your messages ● 53

addresses, address lists and distribution lists ● 58

working with attachments ● 61

using filters and auto-management facilities ● 62

managing spam ● 64

managing messages on the move ● 66

working off-line ● 67

rules of good e-mail management ● 68

summary ● 70

4 e-mail and security

the need for security ● 72

elements of security ● 74

encryption ● 82

attachments ● 85

operational considerations ● 86

choosing a secure e-mail product ● 88

security in practice ● 89

summary ● 92

5 e-mail and the law

general aspects of the law ● 94

questions worth asking ● 96

key aspects of the law ● 98

effective service ● 110

e-mail and company stationery ● 110

taking legal action ● 111

answers to the questions worth asking ● 112

summary ● 114

6 developing a business e-mail policy

the need for a business e-mail policy ● 116

when to create a policy ● 121

what steps to take ● 122

contents

what makes a good policy? ● 124

who to involve ● 127

communicating the policy ● 128

reviewing existing policies and procedures ● 131

beyond a policy ● 133

summary ● 137

7 **creating good messages**

what makes a good message? ● 140

the purpose of your message ● 141

addressing messages ● 142

message structure ● 145

attaching files to messages ● 148

writing clearly ● 152

protecting messages ● 154

other features of e-mail messages ● 154

rules of good e-mail messages ● 157

summary ● 162

appendices

A   finding someone's e-mail address ● 164

B   public key infrastructure explained ● 166

C   example business e-mail policy statements ● 171

D   example disclaimer and confidentiality notices ● 183

glossary ● 187

index ● 195

foreword

Steve Ballmer
President and CEO, Microsoft Corporation

As the world's leading software provider, Microsoft is in the business of delivering innovative products that meet customers' needs. There are many different aspects in doing this, but at the core of it all is effective communication: with customers, with employees and with partners. Good communication is at the heart of success in the business world and our personal lives.

The personal computer has played a major role in the business world – and increasingly in homes and schools – as a means of helping people communicate. In just a few years, e-mail has been transformed from a simple feature for text transfer – available to just a few technology elites – to an essential tool millions of people around the world use daily. The Internet has certainly contributed to its popularity, but that's not the only reason for the incredible growth in its usage.

Businesses everywhere have come to realize that e-mail increases efficiency, speeds information flow, flattens hierarchical structures, encourages collaboration and enables more timely responses to unanticipated situations. It also can be an important internal and external feedback loop.

In his book, *Business at the Speed of Thought*, Bill Gates writes that for the knowledge worker, organizations must 'insist that communication flow through the organization over e-mail so that you can act on news with reflex-like speed'.

Of course, e-mail is not a substitute for face-to-face interactions, which will always play a vital role in how we communicate. But as technology continues to advance, people increasingly expect to be able to communicate anytime, anywhere, on any device.

At Microsoft, we move more than 4 million internal and external e-mail messages a day through our system. It's certainly difficult to imagine life without it, and I know that's true for many other businesses, organizations and individuals.

But as the use of e-mail increases, information overload is also becoming a problem. To help address this, Microsoft recently announced the concept of a 'digital dashboard' – a customized knowledge-management solution based on Office 2000. Its goal is to tame information overload by consolidating personal, team, corporate and external information with single-click access to analytical and collaborative tools – all within one, customizable view from the desktop. This integrated solution will help users quickly to process information that is relevant and critical to their particular responsibilities and then focus on details or take action.

The transformational impact of e-mail on our society is the reason why I am so pleased to contribute to this book, which is about understanding how to use e-mail to make it work for your business. Jonathan Whelan has written this book in a way that shows an in-depth understanding of the position and value of e-mail. It has a logical structure with a good mix of information, pragmatic examples, checklists and a selection of real-life case studies that serve to reinforce the key points in the main text.

e-mail@work gives a rational overview of the strengths and weaknesses of e-mail in a business environment and it offers practical advice which I am sure both new and existing business e-mail users will find invaluable.

January 2000

acknowledgments

This book has been produced with the help of many people who have shared with me their ideas, opinions, comments and knowledge.

In particular I would like to thank Achi Racov who, although an internationally renowned technologist, found time to provide his guidance and expertise on e-mail.

I would like to thank David Engel, Stuart Moffat, Peter Scott, Julian Stainton, Niall Teskey and John Wales, all of whom made a significant contribution. Many other individuals also contributed including Steve Chambers, Christina Coates, Robert Dias, Gerry Fillery, Bruce Greenhalgh, Paul Hester, Peter Howes, David Jordan, Tracey Moore, Stewart Legg, Yaron Ivry and Steve Woods.

Also I am grateful to the many companies who contributed including @rchive–it.com, Alexander Forbes Risk Management, British Airways, British Standards Institution, BUPA, Hertfordshire County Council, Integralis, InTuition, National Westminster Bank plc, Nokia, Rainier, The Marketing & Communications Agency, Theodore Goddard and Western Provident Association. In particular, the expertise of the technologists at Ithaca Solutions Limited was significant.

I should also mention the enthusiasm of Amelia Lakin and her colleagues at Pearson Education.

And finally, the greatest thanks to Dad, David and Rosie, and, of course, to Lindsay and Lizzie, whose encouragement meant that this book actually got finished.

preface

E-mail is no longer just a method of communicating in business, it is a way of doing business.

Nevertheless, like any form of communication, we have to learn to use it wisely.

In less than fifty years computers have redefined the way that we communicate. We are now experiencing a social, commercial and communications revolution of which the Internet is probably the greatest single contributor. The first main use of the Internet was to send text messages (that is, e-mail) and this is still the way that most people use it today.

In the time it takes you to read this preface another 200 people will have connected to the Internet for the first time and will be using e-mail.

❝In the time it takes you to read this preface another 200 people will have connected to the Internet for the first time and will be using e-mail❞

The rapidly increasing use of the Internet, combined with advances in computer technology and the reducing cost of electronic and mobile communications mean that e-mail now sits alongside face-to-face contact, the phone and the fax machine as a primary method of communication. Many businesses already rely on e-mail for their day-to-day operations, for example:

- *Selling products and services.* Many companies now enable their customers to place orders by e-mail.

- *Responding to customer queries.* Most company web sites include the e-mail addresses of various contacts.

- *Communicating with 'field staff'.* Devices such as laptops, palmtops and mobile phones, combined with digital telecommunication networks, enable field staff to stay in touch with base.

- *Distributing information around the business.* Using attachments to distribute information that is in electronic format (such as reports, agendas, spreadsheets and drawings).

- *Marketing and advertising.* Providing automated mailings to existing and potential customers.

- *Projecting the company image.* Communicating with external contacts such as customers, suppliers and business partners.

Although e-mail is a relatively young method of communicating, it has already proved itself to be an effective business tool.

why you should read this book

There is a tendency to treat e-mail as a one-to-one, confidential way of communicating, similar to a phone call, and so take part in informal, unstructured written conversation. But e-mails are not a confidential way of communicating and messages can easily be copied to other people in a context that can make the original content unsuitable, misleading, offensive or legally hazardous.

Exchanging superficial messages, copying jokes to friends and copying messages to others unnecessarily – just because it is easy to do – may seem harmless, but in reality it wastes time and may contain significant dangers. Many businesses have already suffered the consequences of e-mail abuse.

However, it is not enough for businesses to protect themselves from the dangers of e-mail, they must also look to make it work for them.

E-mail is a quick, convenient, easy-to-use, low-cost way of communicating both internally and externally and businesses should use it effectively.

Technology is moving fast and so too is the way that technology is being used. There are already businesses that use software to convert speech to text, eliminating the need even to type their messages and there are businesses who are using advanced pattern recognition technology automatically to read and respond to the messages which they receive.

If you use e-mail in business do you honestly know the answers to the following questions?

- Does your company have a strategy that aims to get the very best out of e-mail while at the same time minimizing the risks of using it?

- Does your company have guidelines covering the use of e-mail? Can you be sure that those guidelines are being followed by your staff?

- What would be the impact on your business if your e-mail system was unavailable for a prolonged period?

- Do you manage your e-mail messages effectively? Do you store them only as

> **"E-mail is a quick, convenient, easy-to-use, low-cost way of communicating both internally and externally and businesses should use it effectively"**

long as you need to? Do you back-up important messages? Can you retrieve backed-up messages if you need to?

There are also specific questions that are asked frequently but the answers are often buried in doubt or jargon. For example:

- Can your e-mail messages be used as evidence in a court of law?
- Should your company e-mail messages contain the same information that is on your company stationery (such as your registered office address and company registration number in the UK)?
- Can you confirm a contract with a customer by sending them an e-mail?
- Do employers have the right to look at the e-mail messages that their employees send and receive?

This book answers these questions and many others. It is a definitive practical guide to using e-mail in business, avoiding the pitfalls and exploiting its potential.

who should read this book

It doesn't matter:

- what sort of business you are in
- whether you are an employer or employee
- what level you are within your organization
- whether you are a frequent or occasional e-mail user
- what sort of computer you use
- which e-mail system you use
- whether you consider yourself to be a computer novice or wizard.

If you use or are considering using e-mail at work, or if you are responsible for staff who use e-mail as part of their work, then this book is for you.

how this book is organized

chapter 1: introduction

Chapter 1 sets the scene for the rest of the book. It discusses the implications of technology on business communications and the role that e-mail has to play in today's commercial world.

chapter 2: a closer look at e-mail

Chapter 2 discusses the key characteristics of e-mail together with its strengths and weaknesses. It covers topics related to e-mail such as speech recognition, video-mail and electronic commerce and looks at the future direction of e-mail.

chapter 3: managing your mail

Chapter 3 looks at the practicalities of e-mail accounts, storing, archiving, retrieving and filtering messages, working with distribution and address lists, attachments and other office-related activities.

chapter 4: e-mail and security

Chapter 4 is devoted to the security needs of e-mail. It identifies the key security risks and suggests ways that you can protect the contents of your messages.

chapter 5: e-mail and the law

Chapter 5 considers the legal status of e-mail and discusses the legal issues which e-mail users face and provides guidance to help you address them.

chapter 6: developing a business e-mail policy

Chapter 6 discusses a business e-mail policy as one way to manage e-mail risks and it provides step-by-step guidance to creating a policy. Sample e-mail policies and disclaimer notices are also included.

chapter 7: creating good messages

Chapter 7 is about writing good e-mail messages. It identifies the characteristics of a good mail message and provides a checklist of questions to ask before you send a message. The focus is on writing effective, professional messages.

using the book

The chapters can be read as a stand-alone text. Each chapter starts with an 'at a glance' section which provides a brief insight into the topics discussed. Therefore you will get a good idea of the content before exploring the detail. At the end of each chapter there is a summary of the key points raised.

At the end of the book there is a set of appendices that provide additional information to the main text and a glossary of the computing terms used.

Dotted throughout the book are examples, tips, watch points and case studies, designed to reinforce the messages contained within the text.

introduction

➤ **at a glance**

the communications revolution

effect of e-mail in business

e-mail as a business risk

making e-mail work for you

e-mail in practice

summary

the communications revolution
from science fiction to reality

" Computers are now so ingrained into our day-to-day lives that it is difficult to imagine life without them "

When the first electronic computer was built in the 1940s its function was exactly what its name suggests, to 'compute'. But today its function is much more than anything that was imagined at that time – except perhaps in science fiction.

We live in a world that depends upon computers. Planes, trains and cars all function with the help of computers. The gas, electricity and water which are delivered to our homes are all controlled using computer technology. In the home our TVs, videos, microwave ovens and other electrical appliances operate using computer technology.

Computers are now so ingrained into our day-to-day lives that it is difficult to imagine life without them. So computers are no longer just calculators. They are business machines, education workstations, games consoles and communication devices. They are no longer huge machines that occupy whole rooms (the first computer was 150 ft wide, 10 ft tall and weighed 30 tons). They are portable devices that slot into bags and jacket pockets. They process text, sound and images and they are used just about any place we happen to be, at work, in our homes and on our travels.

When the first computer was built, the way in which we communicated with each other was face-to-face, by letter, by phone or by telegraph. Today, we still talk face-to-face and on the phone and we write letters and send faxes. However, with the availability of satellites and fibre optic links, businesses can now take part in videoconferencing and send and receive e-mail. In other words, computers have redefined the way that we communicate.

from priceless to affordable

For the same price that you bought a computer a year ago, today you are likely to get a computer with a higher specification. And this has been happening year on year.

> >>> **INFO POINT Moore's law** In 1965 Gordon Moore, one of the founders of Intel, first observed the rate of improvement in the capacity of microprocessors. Moore's law suggests that each new microprocessor contains roughly twice the capacity of its predecessor, and that new processors are launched at intervals of eighteen months to two years.

Because the relative cost of technology is falling every year, the computer is becoming as common as the phone. Before 1945 you could not buy a computer at any price – if you wanted one you had to build your own. By the 1990s, for less than £5 you could buy a wristwatch incorporating a computer that was more powerful than its 30-ton ancestor.

> >>> **EXAMPLE** At the beginning of 1990, a mobile phone in the UK cost a couple of hundred pounds or more. Within the same decade one company was giving them away free at Easter when you bought a chocolate egg – a cost of 40 pence.

from nowhere to everywhere

In the 1940s, if you wanted to make a long-distance phone call, you had to book it in advance with the operator. By accessing the Internet from our own homes, at any time of the day or night we can:

- order a book
- shop for groceries
- buy a tailor-made computer
- book an airline ticket (and choose our seat on the aircraft)
- get information on just about anything imaginable
- send messages to, and receive messages from, any mail address, anywhere in the world.

> >>> **EXAMPLE** On 15 July 1999, British Telecom introduced its first new-age payphone to offer Internet access and e-mail. Access was provided using BT's own e-mail service and it allowed you to sign up there and then.

ff The main reason why people connect to the Internet is to communicate by e-mail JJ

The main reason why people connect to the Internet is to communicate by e-mail. Traditional methods of communication are now converging onto the Internet – text messages, phone calls and video images can all be sent via the Internet. Furthermore, the growth in mobile communications and the continuing improvements in mobile communication devices mean that e-mail is now accessible just about anywhere.

>>> **INFO POINT** 78 per cent of Japanese businesses, 68 per cent of US businesses and 62 per cent of UK businesses have Internet access and use e-mail.
Source: UK Department of Trade and Industry

The rate at which e-mail has been adopted by businesses is a testimony to its value. Because it can improve efficiency, reduce costs and increase productivity and profits, businesses are prepared to welcome it with open arms. In terms of the future use of e-mail, its popularity becomes self-fuelling. More people will use it, so people will use it more.

e-mail business case

>>> **INFO POINT** 86 per cent of all businesses think that information and communication technology is important for business competitiveness.
Source: UK Department of Trade and Industry

So why is e-mail taking the communications world by storm? These are the main reasons.

ff Because e-mail is relatively low cost, convenient, easy and quick, and it is available around the clock, more and more businesses are relying on it JJ

1. *It is relatively low cost*:
   - about the same as the cost of a local phone call to send a message anywhere in the world.

2. *It is easy to copy a message to many people at the same time*:
   - at no extra cost and using only a few key strokes or mouse clicks.

3. *It is easy to distribute information* such as reports, spreadsheets, presentations and other files:
   - just 'attach' them to the messages that you send.

4. *It is convenient*:

   ● it's a 'store and forward' system – you can send and receive messages wherever you are and whenever you want to.

5. *It is relatively quick*:

   ● usually taking only a matter of minutes to travel around the world.

6. *It does not sleep*:

   ● it is available 24 hours a day, seven days a week.

Because e-mail is relatively low cost, convenient, easy and quick, and it is available around the clock, more and more businesses are relying on it.

>>> **INFO POINT** 81 per cent of businesses who use e-mail introduced it to increase their efficiency.

Source: UK Department of Trade and Industry

role of e-mail

E-mail has evolved from being a transporter of simple text messages to being a document sharing and routing facility. Many businesses already use e-mail to improve the way they work and now rely on it for their day-to-day operations.

Table 1.1 shows some examples of how e-mail can contribute to the way you work.

Function	Possible contribution of e-mail
Marketing and sales	<ul><li>providing quotes, product details, company profiles and resumés to customers and potential customers</li><li>taking orders</li><li>producing automated mailings</li></ul>
Purchasing	<ul><li>obtaining quotes and specifications</li><li>placing orders</li></ul>
Operations	<ul><li>transferring data between departments</li><li>communicating internally and externally, nationally and internationally</li></ul>
Design and production	<ul><li>transferring drawings, specifications, schedules, etc.</li><li>reaching decisions more quickly</li></ul>
Customer service	<ul><li>providing general and specific points of contact</li><li>providing an offline 'helpdesk' service</li><li>handling customer queries</li></ul>

Table 1.1
Ways of using
e-mail in business

>>> **EXAMPLE** One well-known Internet bookshop uses e-mail to confirm customers' orders and separately to advise them of despatch details. Additionally, the e-mail address of their customers is used as the customer identifier for future orders. These e-mail messages can be automatically generated and are therefore cost effective, while giving the customers the feel of a very personalized service.

effect of e-mail in business

effect on internal communications

from hierarchies to networks

Traditionally internal business communications were hierarchical, with messages being passed up and down the chain. Managers and directors often used their secretaries and PAs to act as an interface between them and their staff.

However, a move to flatter company structures, combined with an accessible and effective communications mechanism, has revised the model for internal communications.

E-mail has given everyone the power to communicate directly with everyone else and so a communications network has replaced the hierarchical model. Figure 1.1 shows the old and new models.

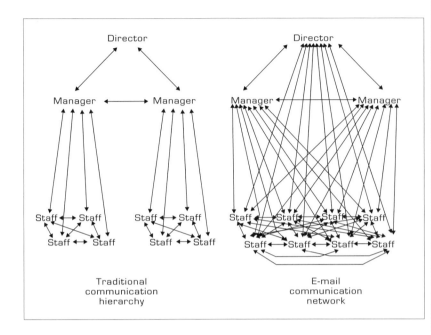

"E-mail has given everyone the power to communicate directly with everyone else and so a communications network has replaced the hierarchical model"

Fig 1.1
The effect of e-mail on internal communications

Employees are now much more empowered. They can communicate up, down and across the organization.

from information 'trickle' to 'waterfall'

Because e-mail makes it so easy to communicate, internal communications have increased dramatically. If you can store the information electronically, then you can attach it to an e-mail message.

Information can now be distributed more quickly and more efficiently around the organization. However, unimportant and even irrelevant information can also be distributed quickly and efficiently. You would never have thought of typing a memo to invite a colleague to lunch, but perhaps without even thinking about it you may send an e-mail.

"An external e-mail message is an advert for your company, in the same way that your company printed stationery is. A good message can portray a professional outfit, a bad one could do more than just create a bad impression – it has landed some companies in court"

The phrase 'information overflow' is often used to describe the volume of information, not all of which is needed. It has even been described as 'information waterfall'.

> **▶▶▶ INFO POINT** Of business e-mail users 27 per cent consider the current level of e-mails they receive to be 'excessive' or 'intolerable'; 41 per cent believe that in five years' time the level of e-mails they receive will be 'excessive' or 'intolerable'.
>
> *Source*: KPMG Consulting

In addition to the volume of messages generated, the volume of information within those messages also contributes to the information waterfall.

Finally, the excessive use of e-mail internally can devalue the information that it is carrying. It can also focus a company on its internal communications rather than the equally, if not more important, external communications.

effect on external communications

E-mail has had a mixed reception in terms of its contribution to external communications.

Few will argue that it helps to establish and maintain relationships with customers, suppliers, partners and others. Many businesses now thrive because of their external e-mail communications and their customers are equally content.

Nevertheless, it can also be frustrating for some people. For those that have been in control of their customer relationships and the primary or even sole contact point, the idea that it is just as easy for someone else in the company to communicate with them can make them feel uncomfortable.

Also, companies have provided training for staff on writing good business letters, accepting that it can help the efficiency as well as the image of the company. However, there are many companies that do not provide the equivalent training for e-mail use.

An external e-mail message is an advert for your company, in the same way that your company printed stationery is. A good message can portray a professional outfit, a bad one could do more than just create a bad impression – it has landed some companies in court. It doesn't matter how many e-mail messages your company sends each day, it can take just one message to ruin your company's reputation.

effect on working practices

Many people seem unavailable to attend meetings or even to answer the phone because they know that they can be reached by e-mail (which they can deal with when they want to). They choose e-mail because it suits them and not necessarily because it is the best method of communication for every occasion. The more e-mails they send, the more they receive, so the more they send, and it soon becomes their preferred method of communicating.

E-mail is not always the best way of communicating. Some things are best dealt with in other ways.

To some people e-mail is an ideal medium in which they can:

- *take part in office politics*

  'I'll copy this to the CEO so that he can see who's really driving this deal forward.'

- *pass the buck*

  'I've forwarded the message to Purchasing so it's no longer my problem.'

- *cover their backs*

  'I've copied the message to Accounts so that I can't be blamed if the bill doesn't get paid.'

These characteristics are not common to all companies. Nevertheless they do occur and e-mail can be a contributing factor.

effect on businesses processes

All businesses operate using a set of processes, either formal or informal, such as:

- raising purchase orders
- submitting tenders and quotations
- chasing unpaid accounts
- managing customer complaints.

E-mail could encourage or even force changes or extensions to your processes.

As an informal process, you may have a secretary who types your letters and you then review and sign them before they go out. But what do you do if those letters are e-mail messages?

As a formal process, in a large organization the raising of a purchase order may rigidly follow a set of predefined steps (for example, completing the form, getting a supervisor's signature, filing a copy of the form in a specific file). Some companies create forms electronically and e-mail them to their suppliers as attachments. There are a number of issues to address:

● What do you do in place of getting a hand-written signature?

● What if the supplier does not have the software to read the attachment?

● How do you link your order to your accounts?

● For how long should you keep the e-mail message that contained the order, and where do you keep it?

And, of course, if your procedures are written down (such as in a 'procedures manual') they will need to be updated.

Although these are not big issues, they will nevertheless need to be thought through. E-mail can change the way that you work. It is even possible to generate messages automatically from business applications.

> ▶▶▶ **EXAMPLE** A unique initiative by the Business & Accounting Software Developers Association (BASDA), has led to the development of eBIS, the electronic Business Interchange Standard, which provides a major opportunity for transmitting invoices directly between accounting systems using e-mail. If this initiative is implemented using an e-mail system which also handles the basic issues of archiving for legal admissibility, good quality proof of receipts for mutual non-repudiation and digital signature, then there is considerable scope to reduce processing costs as well as improving speed and efficiency.

However, although e-mail can be an effective way of communicating with customers, there is a perception that it can be almost effortless.

"E-mail could encourage or even force changes or extensions to your processes"

>>> INFO POINT A study carried out for a high street company revealed that:

- the cost of handling unstructured e-mails is up to 10 times the cost of handling a phone call;

- each e-mail is estimated to take 12 minutes to respond to (18 minutes if the response is reviewed by a supervisor);

- each operator is unlikely to exceed 40 responses per day.

The study also concluded that call centre response staff are excellent at talking to customers – they have had training. Training is also likely to be required to write effective e-mails.

e-mail as a business risk

hidden dangers

Because e-mail is such a powerful tool, it is important that it is used sensibly. You can compare e-mail with a power tool – if it is used sensibly it can be extremely effective. However, in the hands of a novice, or someone who is determined to abuse it, it can be dangerous. E-mail has many hidden dangers:

1. It may be possible for other people to:

   - read or change messages that you send;

   - read, change or delete messages you have stored;

   - change the direction of messages you send.

2. Viruses or other harmful codes can be disguised in files that are 'attached' to messages.

3. 'Chain mail' can choke corporate networks. Like chain letters, chain mail is forwarded onto others, either with the recipient's knowledge or without it (the Melissa virus automatically sends itself to ten addresses which it obtained from the recipient's address book). The result is the same: the creation of a large volume of messages.

> **“** Because e-mail is such a powerful tool, it is important that it is used sensibly **”**

4. Messages can be used as evidence in a court of law.

5. Messages that you think you have deleted may linger in system back-up files.

❝Businesses in particular are vulnerable to e-mail abuse❞

Businesses in particular are vulnerable to e-mail abuse. A message directed outside your company, or by a few key strokes from a disgruntled employee, could mean damaging publicity for your company.

> ➤➤➤ **INFO POINT** Although there is an increasing number of legal cases involving e-mail, the majority of business e-mail users are not aware of the legal and reputational aspects of e-mail.

There are other aspects to e-mail systems that can also be damaging or annoying.

1. You may receive a message but not be able to find out who sent it originally, especially if it has been 'forwarded' on by many people.

2. You may not know if a message that you sent has been received.

3. Jokes, sexist, racist and other offensive material can be distributed easily.

4. You could receive a lot of junk mail (or 'spam' as it is known).

5. Messages can be 'enhanced' with unwanted fancy images, smileys and other features that some people may find more irritating than amusing.

6. Messages may be difficult to read because they are badly written or contain unnecessary content.

7. Messages may be left to linger in the e-mail system, taking up space even though they are no longer required. Conversely, messages (which could be significant business records such as invoices) could be deleted prematurely.

8. Productivity can be adversely affected because of time spent sending or receiving unnecessary messages.

9. People may spend so much time sending and receiving messages that they neglect other important duties.

10. People can hide behind e-mail instead of talking face-to-face or on the phone. An aggressive comment can seem more aggressive if it is put in an e-mail instead of it being said directly to the recipient.

You should think of e-mail as a living entity – it can take on undesirable characteristics. Adding an e-mail system to a chaotic office could just make the situation worse.

reality versus hype

E-mail messages are being used as evidence in legal cases involving businesses. Even companies as big as Microsoft have discovered that e-mail messages sent by their employees can be used years later in legal proceedings against them.

> ➤➤➤ IMPORTANT 'There is a real danger for staff to become overly reliant on technology at the expense of face-to-face communication, hiding behind the technology and creating information overload, inconsistency and miscommunication.'
>
> *The Marketing & Communication Agency Ltd (MCA)*

❝ Adding an e-mail system to a chaotic office could just make the situation worse❞

> ➤➤➤ IMPORTANT 'The vast majority of e-mail messages are effective. They are brief and to the point. They say what they've got to say, then go away.'
>
> **Paul Hester** *Group Messaging Support Manager, National Westminster Bank*

> ➤➤➤ CASE STUDY What is believed to be the biggest action in the UK arising out of defamation by e-mail was settled when Norwich Union publicly apologised in the High Court to a rival private health insurer, Western Provident Association (WPA), and agreed to pay WPA £450,000 in damages and costs.
>
> Legal proceedings began when it was discovered that Norwich Union was circulating damaging and untrue rumours on its internal e-mail system to the effect that WPA was in financial difficulties and being investigated by the DTI.

One bad message can result in mistakes, inefficiency, unwanted publicity, and customer dissatisfaction, all of which can lead to lost business.

Many people rely on e-mail even when other forms of communication would be more appropriate. Few of us would like to be told by e-mail that we are being fired or that we were not going to get the promotion that we thought was 'in the bag'.

>>> **INFO POINT** London-based IT training firm InTuition carried out a survey of a cross-section of 150 small to medium-sized companies who used e-mail. The survey revealed that:

E-mail alters company culture, with users e-mailing each other rather than talking.

81 per cent said that messages were being sent when personal communication would be more effective. They were experiencing impersonal 'management by e-mail'. Managers were overusing e-mail to delegate work or discipline employees.

Many companies discover an unacceptable volume of non-business related messages within their systems and view them as a waste of productive time and misuse of a valuable business resource.

Unsolicited commercial e-mail (also known as 'unsolicited bulk e-mail', 'junk mail' or spam) is one of the scourges of the Internet. Spam is similar to the practice of sending unsolicited conventional mail except that it is significantly less expensive to send spam.

ʽʽ E-mail makes it easy to transmit viruses, knowingly and unknowingly ʼʼ

>>> **INFO POINT** 'Spam' is named after the 'Monty Python' TV comic sketch, first shown in the UK. Set in a restaurant, all the dishes on the menu contained spam – taken from the words 'sp*iced*' and 'h*am*'; spam and chips, spam and eggs, spam and spam. In other words, spam was in everything. (The sketch reflected the widespread availability of spam even in times of rationing during World War II.)

Viruses are much more of a nuisance than spam. They represent a real threat to companies. They include annoying hoax viruses, 'mail bombs' (messages that are intended to disrupt, but which are not necessarily damaging) and destructive viruses intended to cause serious damage by, for example, destroying important files on your PC. In many cases you may not even know that you are transmitting a virus. E-mail makes it easy to transmit viruses, knowingly and unknowingly.

>>> **EXAMPLE** The 'Christmas tree' virus stopped the network of one of the world's largest IT companies for four days. It looked at each recipient's personal address book and forwarded an electronic Christmas card to the first ten names in the list.

However, despite the dangers of e-mail, its growth is a testimony to its value and there is no doubt that by applying appropriate controls you can make it work for your business.

making e-mail work for you

rules of good e-mail usage

To use e-mail effectively does not necessarily mean that you need the latest hardware or software. You can exploit its strengths and minimize its dangers by using common sense.

Many businesses are already using and depending on e-mail. Others are considering it. Whichever category you fall into, there are some fundamental rules that you should follow to make it really work for you.

1. Decide in which ways you can use e-mail to improve your business.

2. Consider how it will fit into the way that your business operates and how you might adapt the way in which your business runs to exploit it.

3. Calculate the costs (tangible and intangible). Bear in mind that the complete life cycle cost of an e-mail message may be many times the preparation and transmission cost.

4. Consider the level of service that you expect to receive (including availability, support, timescales for fault correction and other elements). Your service provider may already have defined their service goals. If appropriate, produce a service level agreement with your service provider.

5. Introduce and update e-mail as part of a long-term strategy for your business.

6. Understand the risks (technical, security, legal, operational, reputational, etc.) and consider ways of minimizing them.

❝ To use e-mail effectively does not necessarily mean that you need the latest hardware or software ❞

7. Write an e-mail policy and guidelines for your staff and give them appropriate training.

8. Continue to monitor its value to your business and be prepared to adapt – changes to technology, the marketplace and your business are always in the pipeline.

> ►►► **IMPORTANT** Without a clear strategy, the addition of new technology just creates more and more channels to exchange information instead of creating processes that really enhance communication. And without standards for using electronic channels, the strengths of accessibility and speed mean that messages can overwhelm the recipient and overtake the sender.
>
> *The Marketing & Communication Agency Ltd (MCA)*

You may already have an established office organization and you may want to fit the e-mail system into your current way of working. Alternatively, you may want to use the introduction, upgrade or replacement of an e-mail system as an opportunity to review the way in which you operate. Whatever the case, you should have a clear strategy.

❝More and more companies are beginning to realize that controlled use is the most effective use of this valuable tool❞

balancing flexibility and control

So e-mail is low cost, convenient, easy and quick. It is available 24 hours a day, seven days a week and more and more businesses are relying on it. But using it also contains hidden dangers. Should you let your employees use it freely, or should you restrict their use of it and, as a consequence, lose many of its benefits? More and more companies are beginning to realize that controlled use is the most effective use of this valuable tool. Fig 1.2 shows the shift in the balance between flexibility and control. The key is to achieve a balance.

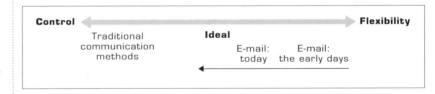
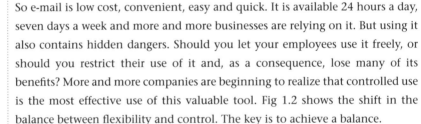

Fig 1.2
Balancing flexibility and control

personal use of business e-mail systems

One of the burning questions that companies ask is: 'Should we allow staff to use our e-mail system for personal use?' The answer is 'Yes' or 'No'! Whether you decide to or not will depend on many factors including:

- how many staff you have
- whether you are giving access to the Internet
- your company culture.

Staff often do not realize that they are 'abusing' their use of the company e-mail system. The e-mail message containing nothing more than office gossip may well have been sent 'innocently' but:

- it takes (company) time to write
- it takes (company) time to read
- it has the potential to damage the reputation of those involved
- it could result in legal action.

> > > **EXAMPLE** Two employees of a US company took legal action against their employer when they discovered that a racist joke was being distributed within the company by e-mail.

Many companies are now realizing the effect on their business of excessive use of personal e-mail at work. Developing a business e-mail policy is the subject of Chapter 6.

policies and guidelines for staff

If you own or run a business you should have policies and guidelines for your staff. You should make sure your staff are aware of these policies and guidelines and you should check that they are being followed. You should also make sure that they are up to date.

An e-mail policy and guidelines can protect your staff and protect your business. Guidelines for businesses should cover:

- the risks and benefits of e-mail to your company
- the legal aspects of e-mail
- security and confidentiality

❝An e-mail policy and guidelines can protect your staff and protect your business❞

- storing and managing messages

- communicating externally

- use of e-mail for personal matters

- possible consequences of ignoring the guidelines.

You should have guidelines for the messages that you write, for example:

- Check that you are sending messages to the right people and that you are not sending messages unnecessarily.

- Do not put anything in a message that you would not want to get into the public domain.

- Do not put anything in a message that you would not be comfortable with being shown as evidence in a court of law.

- Protect yourself, and the people you send messages to, from viruses.

- Have a clear purpose to your messages and make the subject clear.

- Keep messages brief and to the point.

- Make sure your messages are easy to read – by giving them a structure and writing in a language that is clear and concise and avoiding unnecessary jargon.

- Be courteous and friendly.

These basic steps may seem obvious in business communications, but they are ignored with surprising regularity in e-mail messages.

Using e-mail effectively does not just depend on technology. You cannot send messages without the technology, but neither are you likely to get the best use out of the technology unless you use it sensibly.

seven deadly sins of e-mail

Listed below are seven deadly sins of the electronic mail world, together with guidelines to help you avoid them. If you commit one of these sins the consequences may be significant. For example, you may be breaking the law, your Internet service provider may cancel your contract or you may harm or annoy other e-mail users.

▶▶▶ **INFO POINT** An Internet service provider (ISP) is a company that provides Internet services including high bandwidth connectivity to the Internet, e-mail and web hosting facilities.

In this book a 'service provider' can mean an ISP (for Internet e-mail) or, in the case of a company with its own private network and internal e-mail system, the company's IT unit.

1. *Contract*.

   Using e-mail without reading and understanding your e-mail service provider's 'conditions of use'.

   Companies should have guidelines for employees on the use of their e-mail systems. If you cannot find your conditions of use, ask for them.

   ISPs have terms and conditions that you must agree to before you can use their services.

2. *Content*.

   Sending e-mail messages containing material that is illegal, damaging, annoying or which could offend or harm anyone.

   For example, messages containing viruses, sexist or racist material, or copyright material that you do not have permission to reproduce. Also included is chain mail, junk mail, aggressive messages (known as heated messages or 'flames') and messages containing insulting remarks would all fall into this category.

3. *Security*.

   Assuming that e-mail is totally secure.

   Do not include any sensitive information such as personal details or credit card details unless you have protected it or unless you accept that other people may see it.

4. *Viruses*.

   Assuming that messages and attachments are free from viruses and other harmful codes.

   Use up-to-date anti-virus software to protect yourself and others from viruses. Back up important information so that if you do get infected you can revert to those back-ups if necessary.

5. *Identity*.

   Using someone else's e-mail UserId and password.

   Only send e-mail messages using your own e-mail UserId and password (or a UserId and password that has been assigned to you).

6. *Integrity*.

   Changing the content of messages that have been sent.

   If you are forwarding a message that you have received, or sending a message that you had previously sent, do not change the content of the original message.

7. *Privacy*.

   Publicizing someone else's e-mail address.

   Do not advertise, broadcast or give out in any other way someone else's e-mail address unless they have given you their explicit permission. You should treat someone's e-mail address as you would their phone number.

e-mail in practice

This section summarizes the views of Julian Stainton, Chief Executive of Western Provident Association (WPA), about the value of e-mail to his company.

It is an honest account of WPA's experiences of using e-mail as a powerful business tool and highlights many of the issues that companies are facing with their use of e-mail.

>>> **INFO POINT** Western Provident Association is one of Britain's leading health insurers who insure over 500,000 people and more than 5,000 companies.

background

'When I joined WPA in 1987 the business was divided across three, separate locations. It was a business that relied entirely on manual processing – the only form of technology was a single computer that was used for basic accounting and cheque printing. Whether or not it had any other functionality was never discovered because the software running on it was built around an obscure version of proprietary software for which the developers had long since gone out of business.

'It was evident to me that the business needed to be modernized in every dimension, not least from a technological point of view. Yes, in 1987, our standard form of word processing was a manual typewriter and multiple copies required "multi-part sets" – we were Britain's biggest purchaser of multicolour Tippex packs; nothing was ever wasted and a mistake on a multi-part set had to be corrected rather than wasted.

introduction of technology and e-mail

'We approached the IT project from a business perspective, purchasing and building a variety of business applications on Wang VS minicomputers. While these were just a more contemporary version of a mainframe we took the very conscious decision to go for PCs rather than dumb terminals. There were many reasons for this decision, not least of which was the recognition that the PC would become all-powerful at some time in the future and that if we failed to expose people to the benefits of distributed desktop computing then we would be behind the curve for ever more. We had the great advantage of starting from scratch in that more than 90 per cent of our people had never seen or used a computer other than a small number of them who worked in the data input department for claims settlement.

'In hindsight, ironically, the e-mail suite that came with the business application was seen as the ideal "introductory" mechanism to personal computers. We made the conscious decision to make their use both as easy and productive as possible and by the end of the first quarter of 1988 (six months after I joined) the whole business was connected together with a LAN on which the primary traffic was e-mail.

benefits

'The benefits were very substantial. Over three disparate locations we were able to bring an immediate sense of unity coupled with instantaneous information dissemination. All went well and, in turn, the business went from strength to strength.

problems

'Moving forward four years to 1992, e-mail began to pose quite a serious obstacle to our progress. It had become the method of communication. For some it was used as a barrier to keep away from their staff; for others as a sort of "dustbin". It enables, very easily, the instantaneous emptying of your in-tray so that many difficult business issues were simply passed around and around without real responsibility being taken for their resolution.

'The other big problem was the sheer volume of traffic. A very good deal of this volume was made up of what I suppose you would call social use: cars for sale, private diary arrangements and general office chat. If you were out of the office for more than a couple of days there was a good chance that there would be more than one hundred e-mails waiting for you, nearly all of which had no bearing upon the business at all.

lessons learnt

'We learnt some valuable lessons from this: the first was the careful control of the distribution lists with "transmit to all" being withdrawn. We also introduced a special category of e-mail – social, domestic and pleasure (SDP) – that had to be, and is still, used as a prefix on all non-business messages. This excessive use of e-mail, in truth, devalued the power of the medium and the importance of the subjects that it conveyed.

'We have considered, and continue to do so, the exclusive use of internal e-mail for business purposes only and no other. However, organizations are nothing more than organisms that rely upon a community of spirit and information underpinned, of course, by communications. If people fail to utilize the full scope of human communications then their business is likely to suffer. An energetic sports and social club says quite a lot about the health of any business.

'One further problem was rapidly exposed: the complete absence of any typing skills held by anyone apart from those who had trained as secretaries. Circumstances have got no better. While school-leavers have so-called "keyboard skills", few can type properly with both hands. Wherever you go in the UK you see the same thing – be it at a hotel reception desk or in any retail outlet. We've all become masters of the three-finger shuffle! I understand that in America typewriting skills form part of their national curriculum; with the information age, the same should apply here. If I had many wishes – rather than the statutory three – one of those would be to be able to type properly.

'As for the external use of e-mail via the Internet, we have been extremely cautious. This caution was originally driven by our unwillingness to expose ourselves to hacking and other forms of interference on our network. We are so dependent upon our network that any form of corruption is extremely damaging to our business. Our concerns were further reinforced, by an additional dimension, with our cyberlibel action against Norwich Union. The damaging messages transmitted by them were carried on their internal network but served to point up the vulnerability of instantaneous, spontaneous communication, especially when every keystroke is recorded.

bottom line

'To begin with e-mail brought us benefits but over time it became clogged and devalued. Now, having applied suitable controls, it has reverted to a more direct business tool. However, we still recognize the importance of the telephone and consider face-to-face conversation to be the most valuable.'

summary

The growth and popularity of e-mail has brought a new dimension to businesses, not just in the way that they communicate but in the way that they do business.

E-mail offers new opportunities, but to take advantage of those opportunities means more than just using e-mail; it means using it effectively. To use it effectively means:

- understanding its power and the role that it can take on;
- recognizing the effect it can have on the way that you work;
- managing the risks that it presents;
- providing guidance for your employees.

The success of many companies has been built around their use of e-mail. However, despite its great value it does have its drawbacks – the reputation of many companies has been tarnished because of the way employees have used their e-mail systems. Although the majority of businesses introduce e-mail to increase their efficiency, that increase is not guaranteed.

In the world of business, few opportunities appear which do not have risks associated with them – and e-mail is no different. The key is to manage it as you would any other powerful business tool.

a closer look at e-mail

➤ at a glance

e-mail's key characteristics

e-mail and related topics

the future of e-mail

summary

e-mail's key characteristics

Every method of communication has its place but e-mail has proved itself to be a strong contender in many situations, especially in business situations where the communication content tends to be factual and unemotive.

E-mail is a success story but it is not Utopia. It certainly has strengths but it also has its weaknesses. Some of the strengths of e-mail are also contributors to its weaknesses. For example, few people would argue that the ability to send a message to many people simultaneously is one of its greatest strengths. However, this feature also results in the transmission of unnecessary and unwanted messages that can annoy recipients and, in extreme cases, overload corporate networks. The following sections look at each of the main characteristics of e-mail.

ease of use

Once you are connected, sending and receiving e-mail messages is simple. Replying to messages really could not be easier: you click on a Reply button and start typing your reply – the system automatically inserts the address of the person you are replying to in the To: line and inserts a Re: at the beginning of the subject line. If the original message was copied to others, you can reply to all of those who received the original message (by clicking the Reply All button) – the system will include in the Cc: line the addresses of the people who were copied the original message.

When you forward a message you get the chance of including your own message along with the one you are forwarding. So, for example, you can comment on a message and pass the message on to others for them to see your comments as well as the original message.

'Address Books' and 'Distribution Lists' enable you to select addresses

> **"E-mail is a success story but it is not Utopia. It certainly has strengths but it also has its weaknesses"**

from a list of addresses and send messages to a previously specified group, by selecting the group name from a distribution list.

Because e-mail is easy to use, it's easy to pass on information. It's also easy to pass on information that is inappropriate.

>>> EXAMPLE A well-meaning employee was not sure who his audience was, so he sent his message to everyone: 9,000 employees worldwide. As well as the numerous 'Why did you send this to me?' replies, an inexperienced recipient hit the 'Reply All' button.

It is important to make sure that messages are addressed to the correct people. If the e-mail address that you type is not exactly right (that is, each and every character), your message is unlikely to be received. With a letter, you can often make a mistake with the address and get away with it. In fact you can sometimes get away with very big mistakes, such as the wrong town, and still the post gets there – although it might take quite a while to do so.

A wrong mouse click or keystroke could result in your message being sent to the wrong person. If your message contains sensitive information it is easy for others to share it by e-mail. If you dial a phone number incorrectly you find out straight away, but if you type an e-mail address incorrectly it could be days before you find out.

You can attach files to messages by either inserting them or by just 'dragging and dropping' the files from a file (directory) list.

speed

There are two aspects to speed of e-mail:

- speed of creation
- speed of delivery.

speed of creation

Some research suggests that, on average, it takes 30 minutes to write and send a business letter and 5 minutes to write and send an equivalent e-mail message. The time taken to create an e-mail message is typically considerably less than writing a business letter, the main reasons being:

> "Because e-mail is easy to use, it's easy to pass on information. It's also easy to pass on information that is inappropriate"

❝In many cases the pendulum has swung too much towards informality and people write things in an e-mail message that they would not write in a business letter❞

- there is no (or limited) formatting; many business letters require the recipient's address to be placed in a specific location on the paper

- there is no paper handling and therefore no headed paper, envelopes or stamps.

E-mail tends to be treated less formally than a business letter and so people tend to omit some of the formalities associated with business correspondence.

However, in many cases the pendulum has swung too much towards informality and people write things in an e-mail message that they would not write in a business letter.

speed of delivery

Speed of delivery is one of the key strengths of e-mail. You should expect an e-mail to be delivered within minutes, anywhere in the world.

Because you can attach files to messages, you can quickly distribute reports, financial spreadsheets, technical drawings, architect's designs, circuit diagrams, road maps, music, speech, video clips, and just about anything else that you can store electronically, (see 'attachments', p.32).

> ➤➤➤ **EXAMPLE** An editor based in the UK edits financial reports for Far East businesses. At the end of the working day the Far East businesses e-mail their reports to him. He edits them into perfect English and e-mails them back for when the companies return to work in the morning.

cost

The perceived cost of sending an e-mail message to one person is the same as sending it to ten, a hundred or however many you want.

Given that many ISPs do not charge for connection to the Internet, and in some cases there is no charge for the time that you are connected, you could argue that the cost of sending e-mail messages is a matter of pence or even free.

In addition to the cost of sending and receiving messages, you should know the true cost in terms of the total cost of ownership of your e-mail system.

For companies starting from scratch the initial outlay for hardware and software may seem offputting. On the other hand, for a small business with an existing PC, the incremental cost of connecting to the Internet to send and receive e-mail and browse the World Wide Web (WWW), the marginal incremental cost may seem attractive.

For companies with an existing network, e-mail can usually be introduced for an acceptable additional outlay. Even so, there are further costs to consider:

- e-mail server software (such as Microsoft® Exchange® or Lotus® Domino®);
- hardware and software for security functions (such as virus checkers and 'firewalls' to protect against unauthorized access when connecting to the Internet);
- staff to train users;
- staff to administer, support and maintain the service and to provide a helpdesk service.

There are other cost-related elements that are less tangible than the entry costs.

>>> **INFO POINT** E-mail can reduce productivity at work 79 per cent of users look at their messages as soon as they receive them, which disrupts the prioritization of their workload. Their PCs are set to bleep whenever they receive a message.

Source: InTuition

There is a cost in terms of time spent reading poor quality or unnecessary messages. Some people do not always define their audience well and they take a 'blunderbuss' approach – they send the message to everyone and hope to catch the right audience. The result is that a lot of people receive the message unnecessarily and their time is wasted reading it.

Also, the low cost of sending messages, combined with the ease of use, means that unsolicited commercial e-mail (spam) is a consequential evil (see 'managing spam', p.64).

>>> **HOT TIP** 'Many people claim that e-mail increases efficiency and when it is used appropriately that is exactly what it can do. However, when it is used inappropriately it can have the opposite effect.'
Bill Ogley
Chief Executive, Hertfordshire County Council

security

The security of e-mail, or rather the lack of security of e-mail, is often considered to be one of its key disadvantages. It may be possible for other people:

- to read or change messages that you send
- to read, change or delete messages you have stored
- to change the direction of messages you send.

E-mail messages have even been likened to 'electronic postcards'. However, there are two factors that can address this issue of security:

- Not all messages need to be secure. For example, if you send your product catalogue to a customer by e-mail there should be no need to secure it.
- Methods of securing e-mail messages are being introduced into the mainstream. For example, Microsoft® Outlook® allows you to encrypt messages and include a digital signature (which will verify you as being the sender).

Although security products are becoming increasingly available, there is still some effort required to send secure e-mail messages over and above sending ordinary messages. There is an analogy with sending registered letters – you cannot just drop a registered letter in a postbox; you have to take it to the post office and sign for it. So one way or another security can cost time and money.

Also, the threat of viruses contained in e-mail messages has already been discussed. E-mail has shown itself to be a prime vehicle for the transmission of viruses.

accessibility

Today you can access an e-mail system wherever you are, whenever you want. You can do it from the PC on your desk, from your laptop or palmtop or even from your mobile phone. Because the Internet never sleeps, you can send and receive messages any time of the day or night.

"E-mail messages have even been likened to 'electronic postcards'"

As e-mail is a 'store and forward' process, you do not rely upon the recipient being present at their machine or, indeed, even having the machine switched on, before you create and send your message.

➤➤➤ **INFO POINT** It is estimated that more than 100 million users worldwide are connected to the Internet and at least a further 10 per cent are connecting each year.

As with ordinary letter writing, you can take minutes, days or weeks to write your messages, read them through, change or even retype them before you eventually hit the button to send them on their way. Nor are you limited to one recipient. You can address messages directly to more than one person and you can copy (that is CC:) them to others.

Furthermore, as the number of businesses that use e-mail and have access to the Internet are growing, and growing fast, then more businesses are accessible by e-mail. More and more people are using e-mail in their personal lives as well as in business.

If your customers, suppliers and others with whom you communicate are not using e-mail, the chances are that they will be soon.

❝If your customers, suppliers and others with whom you communicate are not using e-mail, the chances are that they will be soon❞

format

You obviously need to be able to type with reasonable proficiency if e-mail is to be anything other than a tedious chore. Here many of the rules and issues that relate to conventional letter writing come into play. You need to be able to express yourself simply and clearly.

➤➤➤ **INFO POINT** E-mail causes misunderstandings, inconsistencies and **problems** 58 per cent of companies feel that e-mail often causes misunderstandings, offence or confusion because people don't think about 'e-mail etiquette' or define rules (an 'e-mail protocol') as to how they will communicate.

Source: InTuition

PCs allow you to copy and paste text between different applications. As long as you are able to 'select' the text, you should be able to copy and paste it. This can be particularly useful if you are writing a message that includes information such as facts or figures, complex words such as medical or scientific terms, foreign words, World Wide Web addresses and e-mail addresses.

If your e-mail system supports other formats in addition to the usual plain text, such as the HTML format, you can send and receive messages in this format (see 'text format', p.147).

However, if your e-mail system does not support other formats you are limited to the keys that appear on a standard keyboard and one font. Having this limitation on the style and layout of your message might appear to be primitive, given that technology is now so advanced. Even so, this limitation can have its advantages. For example:

➤➤➤ **INFO POINT** Hypertext Mark-up Language (HTML) is the computer language used to create the pages that make up the World Wide Web.

- You can avoid wasting time unnecessarily. Some people spend a lot of time on the presentation aspects of word-processed documents.

- Your messages can appear to be less formal than a letter or memo. Letters and business memos can appear formal. You may not want this level of formality. In fact, one of the features of e-mail is that it cuts through this formality.

attachments

❝A great feature of e-mail is that you can attach files to the messages that you are sending❞

A great feature of e-mail is that you can attach files to the messages that you are sending. For example, the whole text of this book, including the artwork, was submitted to the publisher as an attachment to an e-mail message.

➤➤➤ **EXAMPLE** Sheet metal fabricators Allsops's ability to e-mail complex drawings to customers has given them a competitive advantage, especially where customers need work done in a hurry. This and their utilization of other technologies has led to a £2 million increase on their profits.

If you receive a message with attachments, you generally only need to click on the attachment and the system starts the application that is appropriate for the attached file. So if the file is a word-processed document, the system should start the word-processing package on your PC and open the file. Because you have a copy of the files, you can treat them as you do all the other files on your PC.

Most companies find it extremely beneficial to be able to transfer these items within their own offices. In many companies all internal communications have moved to e-mail. Not only has this brought cost benefits in the production and distribution of internal communications, but it has also introduced a form of 'work-flow' control with each employee being 'driven' from a single input queue of work, namely their e-mail inbox.

However, as well as being one of the most popular facilities of e-mail, the ability to attach files is arguably the one that causes the most problems. Common problems include:

❝As well as being one of the most popular facilities of e-mail, the ability to attach files is arguably the one that causes the most problems❞

- attaching files which the recipient cannot open

- forgetting to attach a file when the message said there was a file attached

- the transmission of viruses in attachments

- attaching a lot of files

- attaching unnecessarily large files.

> ➤➤➤ **EXAMPLE** On the day that a contractor reluctantly departed from a large multinational company, he sent a farewell message to every address in the company's e-mail address book. He attached a 100-Megabyte file that brought the company's e-mail servers to a grinding halt.

Sending large attachments can and does cause problems. If you work in a company that has a high-speed network it may be possible to attach documents up to, say, 2 Megabytes. However, if these are being sent to customers who have modems with a speed of 28.8 Kilo bits per second, you can easily occupy their communication capability for an excessive period of time.

However, attachments can and do cause numerous problems for those who receive them. The most common problem is incompatibility: the file cannot be opened because it is not a recognized format. The usual cause is that the recipient does not have the same application or version of application in which the file was created.

> ➤➤➤ **WATCH POINT** Viruses being disguised in attachments can be a serious threat to your organization. Because it is so easy to copy a message, it is also easy to spread a virus, without even knowing that it is happening. Attachments can be carriers for many viruses.

The ability to attach files to messages has led to a dramatic increase in the spread of viruses.

folders

E-mail systems help you to organize your messages using 'folders'. As with most PC filing systems, you can store, retrieve, copy, move and delete messages in those folders.

In addition to the standard folders ('Inbox','Outbox', 'Sent mail', 'Deleted mail'), you can usually create your own folders and give them meaningful names such as Orders, Complaints, Minutes and so on.

Messages are usually listed in the folder so that you can see all the messages, including the address of the person who sent the message, its subject and the date and time when it was received. Many systems are flexible enough to allow you to sort the order in which the messages are listed on the screen; for example, you can sort them by sender, by subject or by date received.

However, because folders make it easy to store and manage messages, some people treat their e-mail systems as long-term message stores. This can cause problems to private (company) e-mail systems and may result in:

- a slowing down of the e-mail system – message files become clogged;

- additional costs – increased storage and system maintenance;

- inadequate back-up of important information – the e-mail system may not receive the same level of back-up as other information stores.

The ability to store and manage messages is a very useful facility of e-mail systems and, as with any resource, common sense should be applied to its use. Many companies include in their e-mail policies specific guidelines for their staff regarding the use of folders for storage.

e-mail and related topics

e-mail, the internet and the world wide web

the internet and the world wide web

The Internet has taken e-mail from being a valuable business tool to an invaluable business asset.

❝Many companies include in their e-mail policies specific guidelines for their staff regarding the use of folders for storage❞

> **>>> EXAMPLE** Leez Priory offer a wedding venue service which they advertise on their web site. Of their business 30 per cent is now generated through e-mail enquiries. The conversion rate from e-mail enquiry to actual sale is greater than any other enquiry channel – and the e-mail enquiries are a quicker process.

Despite the perceived deficiencies of the Internet (such as the lack of a single governing body, no service level guarantees and the lack of a robust, practical and universally agreed security framework) it goes from strength to strength.

The World Wide Web (WWW) has extended significantly the value of the Internet to businesses. Browsers such as Microsoft® Internet Explorer® and Netscape® Navigator® combined with hypertext links – clicking on highlighted text and graphics to link to related material or sites – make access to information almost effortless.

Many people now expect companies to have a web site. Companies publicize the address of their web site on their company stationery and advertisements.

e-mail and your company web site

E-mail goes hand in hand with your web site. Here are some of the main influences that your web site can have on your company's e-mail:

1. Providing answers to 'frequently asked questions' (FAQs), thus reducing queries made by e-mail (and phone, fax, letter).

2. Guiding viewers to the right part of your business: giving specific e-mail addresses (such as 'helpdesk' or 'sales') to direct customers to the correct department and hence reducing the need to pass messages around internally in your company.

3. Providing structured (formatted) input to your company using forms with, for example, pre-formatted fields, 'drop down' boxes and 'option buttons' can be used for a wide range of purposes such as:

   * customer orders

❝E-mail goes hand in hand with your web site❞

- customer feedback

- market research.

❝However, it is not enough to have a presence on the web; customers may expect a response to their e-mail messages within a reasonable timeframe❞

Where a response to a query by e-mail could result in a lengthy message and attachments, a brief response with a pointer to your web site could be a preferred option for the customer as well as for the company.

Similarly, to inform customers of your company news, offers or other items of interest, a brief reminder to visit your web site could avoid lengthy messages. Some companies e-mail their customers with a few headline sentences of information that may interest them and include the web page address (that is, the Uniform Resource Locator, URL) of where they can find more detailed information.

However, it is not enough to have a presence on the web; customers may expect a response to their e-mail messages within a reasonable timeframe.

Between March and July 1999 marketing communications consultancy Rainier Limited carried out a survey of the FTSE 100 companies to gauge the speed of response to messages sent to e-mail addresses given on the companies' web pages. Fig 2.1 summarizes the results of the survey.

▶▶▶ INFO POINT Only 58 per cent of companies responded to an investor query from their web site.

Source: Rainier Limited

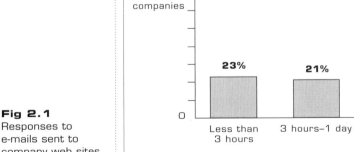

Fig 2.1
Responses to
e-mails sent to
company web sites

    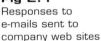

>>> **HOT TIP** 'Having a web site without a direct feedback mechanism is like having a freephone help line, but no receptionist.'

Stephen Waddington
Director, Rainier Limited

Following the survey it was suggested that an acceptable response time is under three hours. However, a response during the next working day may be acceptable in many situations.

e-mail, intranets and extranets

intranets and extranets

>>> **INFO POINT** Intranets (internal Internets) provide all the benefits of Internet technology with the added benefit of security. They use the same technology (browsers, web servers, TCP/IP, HTML, etc.) but are confined to private (company) networks.

An Extranet is an Intranet that has been extended so that some or all of its content is accessible to selected external parties. For example, you may give access to some customers who will benefit from the information that is available.

An Intranet can significantly reduce the volume of internal e-mail traffic. Departments can have their own sites and up-to-date information can be shared without the need to send e-mail messages. Many people question the need for 'broadcast messages' (that is, messages sent to all users) when an Intranet exists.

With e-mail the information is fed to the recipient whereas with an Intranet it is up to the recipient to go in search of it. As a consequence there is a need to train users to fetch information rather than being fed it – and of course the same can be said of your web site.

Rather than attaching a file to a message destined for, say, fifty people, you could consider:

- putting it on your Intranet

- sending an e-mail message which includes the Uniform Resource Locator (URL, that is, the location of the Intranet page) or the location in a shared directory of where the information can be found.

There are many other benefits of an Intranet but these go beyond the scope of this book.

"An Intranet can significantly reduce the volume of internal e-mail traffic"

e-mail, newsgroups, mailing lists and chat rooms

newsgroups

>>> **INFO POINT** A Newsgroup is an electronic discussion group, organized by topic. You can subscribe and send messages on any of the topics and view the contributions of others. You can access your chosen Newsgroups using your normal Internet browser or through specific Newsgroup reader software – usually bundled with the ISP's software.

Newsgroups can be a useful source of information from a very wide community. However, they can also:

- increase your e-mail traffic
- be used for personal interest
- increase the risk of legal action.

An employee might express their views which may be assumed to be the views of your company because they were submitted using a company e-mail address. Consequently some companies now insist that a disclaimer is included in the signature portion of messages sent to Newsgroups.

mailing lists

>>> **INFO POINT** A mailing list is a server which copies mail on a particular topic to all those users who have subscribed to that topic.

Mailing lists are different to address lists (which are discussed on p.60). There are different types of mailing list:

❝ Like Newsgroups, Mailing lists can be a useful business facility, but they can also increase e-mail traffic and be used for personal purposes**❞**

- *active*: subscribers can post messages;
- *passive*: only the owner of the list can post messages;
- *moderated*: someone reviews and, if necessary, filters the messages;
- *unmoderated*: no review or filtering takes place.

Although a Mailing list is very similar to a Newsgroup in operation, it usually lacks the ability to show the whole thread of discussion.

Like Newsgroups, Mailing lists can be a useful business facility, but they can also increase e-mail traffic and be used for personal purposes.

chat rooms

>>> INFO POINT A Chat room is a system that enables users to have an interactive (real-time) typed conversation. What you type on your PC is seen at the same time by the person or people with whom you are communicating and vice versa.

Chat rooms can be a useful way of obtaining information from customers and providing some services (for example, on-line help) for which the store-and-forward nature of e-mail can result in a long sequence of e-mail messages over a protracted period of time.

However, chat comments are ordered in time sequence so it can be difficult to follow multiple threads of discussion within the room.

e-mail, groupware and workflow

>>> INFO POINT **Groupware** is a set of technology tools that lets businesses share information.

Workflow relates to the automation of business processes. It allows a business to use tools accurately to describe their business processes in terms of tasks, policies, skills and service levels. The tools then support the processes by capturing, distributing, managing and monitoring work items according to the rules defined for the processes.

Groupware and Workflow are most commonly employed in larger organizations.

Both Groupware and Workflow need similar supporting technology and both can involve e-mail.

Some products include e-mail as an integral part of the system; others consider it as an additional (but collaborative) element. Two of the most common features of many systems are:

1. *Document management*: storing documents centrally can avoid duplication, reduce message traffic and make sure that the most up-to-date information is available.

   Some products provide full Workflow support. That is, they support the automated sharing, routing and control of documents for the people who need to work on them.

2. *Diary management*: a key ingredient of this feature is the ability to schedule meetings between several people. The system examines the diaries of all the nominated attendees and suggests times when they are all available. The person scheduling the meeting chooses the time most suitable and then, at the click of a mouse, the system will despatch e-mail messages to all attendees to advise them of the meeting, its time and its venue. The recipients are each given the option to accept or refuse the invitation. If they accept then the recipient system causes an entry to be placed into their own diary record giving the details as advised in the e-mail message, and generates a reply message to the person setting up the meeting.

e-mail, speech synthesis and speech recognition

>>> **EXAMPLE** UK-based ISP Freeserve offers a 'Speechmail' service which allows you to access your e-mail using a telephone. You can listen to your messages and even reply to them over the phone, without even needing to switch on your computer!

speech synthesis

Speech synthesis (or text-to-speech, TTS) is the conversion of text to artificial speech. The technology has existed for many years and there are commercial packages available.

The synthesis of the human voice is a well-understood technology, albeit one that, in its cheaper forms, tends to create voices that sound like a drunken robot. The technology now offers a choice of accents and genders through the manipulation of the various parameters controlling the speech generation.

Apart from some obviously artificial intonation, TTS systems are prone to mispronunciations, particularly of names, which is another good reason not to have them address your customers directly. They will have a shot at pronouncing anything that looks like a word and will read out or spell apparent gibberish. This gibberish may be valid business data, such as references or invoice numbers. A scan of your typical e-mail messages will reveal their suitability for being read out aloud.

A number of applications are available that can read e-mail messages and vocalize them. This is a very useful feature for the visually impaired which opens up e-mail as a channel of communication that might otherwise be unavailable to them.

speech recognition

Speech recognition addresses one of the major drawbacks of e-mail, namely the relatively slow input method: typing. The spoken word is turned into a textual representation.

Although speech recognition is more complex than speech synthesis (with the dependence on understanding diction, accent and context), it has received much attention in recent years. Commercial packages are available at a range of prices and performance. Most systems have to be 'trained' for each individual user if a large recognition vocabulary is to be available and a high degree of accuracy is required.

Voice processing technologies do not yet make the ideal interface to e-mail, but they will increasingly provide an effective and useable interface which will suit many circumstances.

> **❝ For users of e-mail who may have difficulty typing, speech recognition software can be a significant benefit ❞**

>>> **EXAMPLE** A lawyer who was interviewed dictates her e-mail messages to her secretary who then types and sends them. She said that it was much quicker than typing them herself, especially for long messages. A good candidate for speech recognition software perhaps?

Not only can speech recognition software be used to dictate messages but the software can also be configured to drive the e-mail application as well as taking the dictation of the message content. So, for example, the software could be commanded to 'send an e-mail to Mike Bloggs at HisCompany dot com' and it would open the e-mail application, create the 'To:' line of an e-mail message as 'mike.bloggs@hiscompany.com' and then be ready to take the rest of the message.

For users of e-mail who may have difficulty typing, speech recognition software can be a significant benefit.

Video-mail
can be thought
of as an
extension to
e-mail – it is
pictures and
sound, not
text; you see
and hear the
person who
sent you the
message

e-mail and video-mail

Video-mail can be thought of as an extension to e-mail – it is pictures and sound, not text; you see and hear the person who sent you the message.

Multimedia communications have had limited application so far, largely due to the cost of bandwidth, that is, the capacity of the communications link which is usually a phone line. This tends to limit the market to major corporate organizations.

However, there are several factors that now make the technology and its application more widely accessible to all businesses:

- continued improvements in compression algorithms – squeezing more data into the same space, or bandwidth;

- more powerful PCs with multimedia capability and video decoders as standard;

- better integration of digital equipment – PCs, palmtops, TVs, etc.;

- reduced costs in real terms.

Even today receiving video clips requires no more than a standard PC; no special software or expensive hardware is necessary.

The main benefit to businesses is the 'weight' of a video-mail. A message from a salesman to a potential customer could well have more effect if it is visual. But video-mail is not a replacement for text-based e-mail. Like other forms of communication it has its place.

e-mail and electronic commerce

For most businesses electronic commerce (e-commerce) means trading over the Internet. It is the buying and selling of goods and services and all the related activities, such as the transmission of payments for those goods and services, marketing, communication and customer support.

Although e-commerce is beyond the scope of this book it cannot be totally ignored as it is one of the significant drivers that has contributed to the spread and success of present day e-mail systems.

You can even think of e-mail as being a soft introduction to e-commerce; by using e-mail you can initiate, negotiate and agree a contract with a customer or supplier.

>>> **EXAMPLE** A major UK savings bank has announced that in future it will only accept deposits from investors who will operate their accounts over the Internet where their e-mail address will form their basic identifier. The justification is that Internet transactions cost only a fraction of that of transactions generated by other means.

❝E-mail is past its infancy, but only just❞

the future of e-mail

Although the use of e-mail has grown phenomenally in the last few years, the technology and the way it is put to use in business still has considerable scope for development. E-mail is past its infancy, but only just. Developments continue in four key areas:

>>> **IMPORTANT** The phenomenal success of mobile phones, laptop computers and the Internet has created an urgent need for wireless connections, providing the freedom to communicate and work anywhere, anytime. The convergence of telecommunications and computing is producing a new generation of devices that communicate seamlessly over networks and integrate media, telephony and computing.

Nokia

- e-mail software

- communications standards (or protocols)

- telecommunications

- devices, such as PCs and Personal Digital Assistants (PDAs).

In theory, developers supply what users need. In practice, there are many factors that dictate what actually gets delivered to the market:

- industry standards – what is or will be recognized as acceptable or universal.

- user requirements: and what users can reasonably expect to have.

- technology capability: what the technology can actually achieve.

- development costs: the cost of producing the product.

- demand: a market willing to buy.

The remaining part of this chapter focuses on five aspects in which tangible changes are likely in the coming years.

1. Mobile phones and PDAs as e-mail terminals.

2. Unified messaging: the integration of e-mail with voice and other messaging systems.

3. Enhanced message management.

4. Security.

5. Legislation.

Each of these areas is discussed in the following sections.

>>> WATCH POINT When you are considering new technologies and services, there are a number of factors that you should bear in mind, as you should with any system. For example:

● migrating from existing systems (including folders, back-ups, address books and any supplementary systems and services that you use)

● interfacing with other systems (internal, customer, supplier and other external systems)

● migrating to future systems

● getting tied into a potentially limiting technology

● getting locked into a particular vendor.

>>> INFO POINT 86 per cent of UK businesses use mobile phones.
Source: UK Department of Trade and Industry

mobile phones and PDAs as e-mail terminals

Ordinary mobile phones can be awkward devices from which to type messages as they do not have a suitable keyboard. But a combined mobile phone with a useable alpha keypad, e-mail, web browsing and other applications (including the ability to run your own custom applications) could be a valuable business tool.

One development that suggests that e-mail and other Internet features will gain importance in the mobile world is the increasing effort being put into the development of Personal Digital Assistants (PDAs) incorporating mobile telephony.

>>> WATCH POINT If you send messages to mobile devices you should take account of their current limitations. Compared to desktop PCs and landlines, mobile devices have:

● limited display capabilities

● reduced application functionality

● higher transmission costs.

Although as yet there are no universal standards covering the wider potential of mobile phones as a PC-like terminal, many manufacturers are collaborating to create (de facto) 'open' standards for mobile communications devices. For example, the Wireless Application Protocol (WAP), which is already available commercially, enables remote access through mobile handsets to e-mail, accounts, group calendars, message boards and other corporate Intranet applications.

At a time when the global future of mobile telephony standards is still far from certain, it is too early to say which standard will ultimately prevail. In the meantime there is likely to be more than one to choose from.

unified messaging

> **▶▶▶ INFO POINT** Unified Messaging is the integration of e-mail with voice, video and other messaging systems.
>
> It offers the prospect of a universal Inbox for all your messages, whether received by phone, e-mail or even fax, accessible by any appropriate device.

❝Unified Messaging provides an effective answer to the problem that comes from having separate systems and mailboxes for text, voice and images❞

Unified Messaging provides an effective answer to the problem that comes from having separate systems and mailboxes for text, voice and images. The current separation is inefficient from a technological, organizational and personal viewpoint and inefficient and cumbersome for users.

With a Unified Messaging System you get a single Inbox to which all your messages (text, voice, fax and image) are directed. The PC is the ideal machine from which to check your Inbox, as it can handle all the media types that can be thrown at it. It is a true multimedia device and it also gives you access to the other business systems you may need in order to frame your responses. But away from home or the office, you may not always have access to it. The potential of mobile phones and related devices for handling mail on the move has already been discussed, but there is also scope to handle e-mail from an ordinary phone using voice recognition and text-to-speech systems.

> **▶▶▶ IMPORTANT** In 1998 there were approximately 850,000 people using unified messaging services. By 2003 the number of users will have risen to almost 100 million and by 2006 to 170 million users.
>
> By 2006, unified messaging will be well along the path to universality. Three-quarters of businesses will either use unified messaging services, or deploy their own equipment to provide equivalent capabilities.
>
> Ovum

For Unified Messaging to gain widespread acceptance, there are several factors to consider in addition to the integration of a set of hardware and software components which are currently separate. These factors include:

- *contact management*: preferences for the way in which your company contacts customers

- *message and process management*: workflow, conversations (that is, the exchange of many related messages) and storing messages

- *flexibility*: vendor independence (or acceptable dependence) and the ability to adapt as requirements change and products develop.

message management

❝It may be that for good reasons you are unwilling or unable to treat an e-mail message as a substitute for a paper original – the 'electronic original'❞

In the same way that many businesses now have telephone 'call centres' we can expect to have e-mail 'call centres'. Software to support these centres will need to be developed or extended to manage:

- *workflow*: the routing and control of messages;

- *conversations*: the exchange of many messages on the same topic, each of which might be handled by a different operator;

- *message retention and retrieval*: storing messages for audit and legal purposes.

E-mail messages received today are often not handled effectively and tend to be treated differently by individuals within an organization – even if there is an effective and well-policed e-mail policy. It may be that for good reasons you are unwilling or unable to treat an e-mail message as a substitute for a paper original – the 'electronic original'.

While you will still need to make sure that you implement good business processes, you can expect to see products in the future that will enable you to manage your messages in a straightforward manner. There might be significant cost savings if important messages were:

- automatically retained and archived at the point of transmission and point of receipt;

- automatically stored for the required length of time without human intervention;

- retained using systems that allowed simple and effective searching;

- held in a manner that provided 'electronic original' status.

There are products now available which enable users to develop trust in their established systems, making it possible to move from today's informal use of e-mail to e-commerce and remain confident in the 'electronic original'.

security

Many people suggest that current security facilities such as digital signatures and digital certificates are not yet sufficiently widespread and can be difficult to use. (See Chapter 4 for more details of these facilities.)

As common security features are now becoming an integral part of many e-mail systems and are underpinned with a maturing infrastructure, we can expect more extensive use of them. As more business is transacted by e-mail we should expect to see increased demand for more common and user-friendly security products integrated with e-mail systems. Furthermore, inherently trust-worthy organizations such as banks, government departments and post offices may well consider offering security services, which in turn may give businesses confidence to use e-mail more extensively.

legislation

With the growing importance of Internet e-mail and its potential to impact national economies, governments are increasingly keen to make sure that any impact will be favourable. They are therefore legislating in ways that should help you to develop business via e-mail.

Although legislation is often specific to territories, it is either in place or can reasonably be expected in the following areas:

- spam

- viruses

- content filtering

- digital signatures

- encryption

- electronic original.

Whereas the Internet is perceived as being a truly modern phenomenon allowing the creation of new business models, many of the underlying supporting requirements remain unchanged. As with the postal service, an e-mail message could be anything from an informal note to an invoice to a contract to a writ. In many cases the proposed legislation should be able to draw on history and align electronic practice with its paper-based equivalent.

summary

Every method of communication has its place but e-mail has proved itself to be a strong contender in many situations, especially in business situations where the communication content tends to be factual and unemotive. But e-mail is just one of the ways of communicating – you should not assume that it is always the best.

The frequently quoted strengths of e-mail (such as its ease of use, speed, cost and accessibility) can also make it easy for e-mail to be abused. Junk mail thrives, productivity can be adversely affected and the spread of viruses is now measured in hours as opposed to days (as it was before the existence of the current e-mail systems and the Internet).

E-mail is no longer considered as an isolated messaging tool. It goes hand in hand with the Internet and Internet technologies, which in turn makes Newsgroups, Mailing lists and other facilities accessible. Furthermore, continuing developments in many areas including video-mail, text-to-speech and speech recognition show that e-mail is far from standing still.

It is probably safe to assume that anything that can be done now with e-mail will also be done in the future – but it will be easier, faster, less expensive, more robust and more efficient. Lower cost, higher specification hardware, more bandwidth and faster transmission will all contribute to make e-mail an even more effective business tool.

managing your mail

> **at a glance**

why manage your mail?

managing your messages

addresses, address lists and distribution lists

working with attachments

using filters and auto-management facilities

managing spam

managing messages on the move

working off-line

rules of good e-mail management

summary

why manage your mail?

Many companies direct their efforts at selecting an e-mail technology, and install it without giving enough consideration to the way they will use and manage their messages.

Most people are aware that the real cost to a business of sending a letter is significantly higher than the cost of the stationery and postage, but they are not aware of the additional costs of e-mail beyond the obvious technology cost. But cost is not the only reason to consider message management. You should also consider the need:

● to archive messages that you have received and sent;

● to retrieve archived messages;

● to comply with statutory and regulatory requirements;

● to integrate with your existing business systems and processes, or changes to those processes to accommodate your use of e-mail.

Also, not looking after your e-mails can have the following effects:

● You could be wasting disk storage space and so possibly have to spend time and money on unnecessary machine or storage upgrades.

● The response time of your PC or message server could slow down affecting your ability to do business in a timely manner.

● You can waste time searching for messages which you may or may not have stored.

In certain cases, poor message management can even lead to loss of service. Some company systems have ground to a halt because their message files have been so full.

"Many companies direct their efforts at selecting an e-mail technology, and install it without giving enough consideration to the way they will use and manage their messages"

Also, your service provider will monitor the e-mail system and will act to make sure that the storage space used and the volume of e-mail traffic is kept to reasonable levels. This helps to make sure that all users of the e-mail system receive an acceptable level of service. Refer to the 'conditions of use' of your e-mail service provider or, if you use a private network, ask your IT support unit.

good management practice

Just because the communication mechanism is electronic there is no reason not to apply tried and trusted management techniques to the management of your e-mail. The more you use e-mail, the more important it is that you manage it and therefore your time effectively.

> **▶▶▶ INFO POINT** UK directors spend 11 per cent of their time – over five working weeks a year – reading and answering e-mail.
> In total, UK directors devote over 75 million days a year to dealing with e-mails, an average of 5.2 weeks per director.
> *Source*: KPMG Management Consulting

Most e-mail systems come with folders and other facilities that allow you to manage your e-mail messages. You should take advantage of these facilities and you should also follow some simple steps that are discussed in this chapter.

In the UK the British Standards Institute (BSI) DISC (Delivering Information Solutions to Customers) has published a Code of Practice titled *Legal Admissibility and Evidential Weight of Information Stored Electronically* (PD 0008:1999). This provides a useful baseline when developing your e-mail storage needs. DISC is the part of the British Standards Institute for standardizing information and communications technology.

❝ The more you use e-mail, the more important it is that you manage it and therefore your time effectively ❞

management standards

In the words of the Code itself:

> The Code describes the means by which it may be
> demonstrated at any time, in a manner acceptable in a court of
> law, that the contents of a specific data file created or existing
> within a computer system have not changed since the time of
> storage, and that where such a data file contains a digitized
> image of a physical source document, the digitized image is a
> true fascimile of that source document. The issue being
> addressed is essentially one of authentication.
>
> (PD 0008:1999 p.13)

The Code goes on to say:

> Irrespective of issues of legal admissibility or evidential weight,
> the Code defines best practice for electronic storage of business
> or other information. As such, complying with its
> recommendations is of value to organisations even when
> evidential issues are not relevant.
>
> (PD 0008:1999 p.13)

The policy includes the following topics:

● information management policy

● duty of care

● procedures and processes

● enabling technologies

● audit trails.

66 Managing
your mail
means more
than just
managing your
messages;
you should
also consider
the service
that you
receive 99

role of your service provider

Your service provider may have defined in their 'conditions of use' rules which
relate to the management of your messages. For example, they may automatically archive messages that are more than, say, three months old. Therefore, you
should check with your service provider what their procedures are and also
what they expect of you.

Managing your mail means more than just managing your messages; you should also consider the service that you receive. If you use, or intend to use an ISP, you should make sure that you are happy with the level and type of service offered. Although price may be important, it should not be the sole factor for a business.

managing your messages
working with folders

Some people will say that your e-mail system is a messaging system and that the folders are a temporary store for your messages and should not be used for storing important information. Others will say that your e-mail system comes with an efficient means of storing your messages so it should be utilized to the fullest.

So which point of view is correct? The answer is both. However, the key is to maintain a sensible limit to the number of folders and a sensible number of messages in each of those folders. Something like 10–20 folders at a given level and up to 100 messages in a folder are useful starting points for limits.

Before setting up folders, you should:

- think about the type and number of folders that you will need;
- consider how those folders relate to your existing office practices and your own working practices;
- check with your service provider for any guidance they may have.

You should consider the folder structure from as many operational aspects as possible. Even though the structure can be changed and messages transferred to different folders, this can be a significant task in large busy offices with many folders and many customers.

The majority of e-mail systems come with a standard set of folders. The creation of additional folders and the way you store your e-mail messages will depend on the way in which your office stores other records and also on the way in which you use e-mail.

For example, if you only use e-mail for internal communication it may be sufficient to keep a copy of your e-mails for a minimum of 30 days and leave

❝You should consider the folder structure from as many operational aspects as possible❞

**ff E-mail does
not remove the
need to keep
records, but
you must make
sure that your
existing
procedures are
extended to
cover e-mail"**

it at that. A 30-day period allows backtracking of most business problems without requiring too much formality or storage space. On the other hand you may wish your sales people to keep records of each quarter's sales returns for at least four whole quarters to allow comparisons with last year's results.

The way in which you store e-mail messages may depend on the way in which you presently organize your office. E-mail does not remove the need to keep records, but you must make sure that your existing procedures are extended to cover e-mail.

storing, backing up, archiving and retrieving messages

First, here is a definition of the terms in this section's title.

- *Storing*: saving your messages (in folders in your e-mail system, on your client PC or on a server).

- *Backing up*: keeping a copy of your messages in case your originals get damaged.

- *Archiving*: moving your messages to a long-term store.

- *Retrieving*: accessing (reading) your backed-up or archived messages.

BSI's DISC document *Legal Admissibility and Evidential Weight of Information Stored Electronically* (PD 0008:1999) provides a useful baseline when developing your e-mail storage requirements.

▶▶▶ **WATCH POINT** Wherever you decide to store your messages you should make sure that:

- you have an appropriate back-up;

- you remember to save any attachments which may have been sent with the messages;

- you protect messages and attachments that contain sensitive information, for example, by encrypting them;

- you can retrieve them and that you can do so within an acceptable timeframe.

If your messages are stored on a central e-mail server, they may be backed up by your System Administrator or IT support team, but do not assume that this is so. If you are in any doubt, check by asking them.

If you do not have a System Administrator or IT support team, then you probably need to run your own back-ups. You should consider the impact on your business if you lost your messages. This impact, together with the volume of messages that you archive, will determine the economic frequency with which you should run your back-ups.

"When you back up or archive messages think about how you will retrieve those messages"

>>> **INFO POINT** Some e-mail packages will perform a regular archiving cycle of old messages into an archive area that you can specify. This feature, coupled with a regular back-up cycle for your PC, could provide adequate back-up for your e-mail.

Even a small office should probably run a back-up at least once a week. You should also think about where you store your back-up copies and archives. For fire security and disaster recovery considerations you should ideally store your back-ups in a separate building away from where the original copies of the messages are stored.

When you back up or archive messages think about how you will retrieve those messages. A lot can happen between archiving and retrieving a message. For example:

● you may have changed your e-mail system;

● you might have moved to a different office location;

>>> **WATCH POINT** Whatever mechanisms you use to back up, archive and retrieve your messages, you should test them fully to make sure that they do in fact work. If you are in any doubt you should get professional advice.

● you may be using a different support unit.

Many e-mail systems now come with facilities that help you to search for messages that you have stored in folders. There are also independent products that can help you search for messages that you have stored within and outside your e-mail system (such as on a shared server). There are even products that are designed to search your messages and create an index of them which you can browse.

trusted third party archiving

Some service companies are now offering to take a back-up copy of your data and store it securely on their servers. The service will usually guarantee to keep the data safe and only to permit the correctly identified owner to have access to it.

If you decide to use a trusted third party there are a number of factors that you should consider, for example, you should:

● check that they have a good reputation – if necessary ask for references;

● ask them to confirm that they will comply with all necessary legislation;

● check that the level of protection offered is adequate for your needs. Consider encrypting your data before transmitting it to them so that the possibility of any unauthorized party having sight of the details is greatly reduced;

● agree with them the level of service that will be provided (including availability and retrieval times).

After all, you are trusting them with your important business data.

❝ You should only keep messages for as long as you need to. In other words, delete any messages that you no longer need❞

> ►►► **WATCH POINT** Be careful about using services such as these. Make sure that you are completely satisfied with the bona fides of the provider.
>
> It would also be prudent for you to encrypt your data prior to transmission so that the possibility of any unauthorized party having sight of the details is greatly reduced.

deleting messages

You should only keep messages for as long as you need to. In other words, delete any messages that you no longer need. Although you have deleted messages from your folders, they may still linger. For example, there may be copies stored on your back-up files and your archive files. There could also be copies stored in the sender's PC, back-up files and archive files – but of course there is little you can do about this.

managing deleted messages

Why should you be interested in messages that you have deleted? Although you may have 'deleted' them, they might still be in your mail system. In some systems, if you delete a message it is moved from the folder it was in to a 'Deleted items' folder. The 'Deleted items' folder acts as a safety net as it allows you to recover messages that you deleted in error.

However, there comes a point when the 'Deleted items' folder itself must be emptied and the messages truly deleted. Some e-mail packages give you the option automatically to delete these items when you exit the package. This can be a very good option to select, but be aware that if you inadvertently exit the package in the middle of the day then your 'Deleted items' will get cleared at that time.

Some systems can be configured automatically to delete the contents of the 'Deleted items' folder periodically (for example, daily, every three days or weekly) and the user can specify the periodicity.

managing your in-tray

You should manage your e-mail in-tray (Inbox) in a similar way to your paper in-tray. For example, you should:

- set aside specific periods in your day to look at your messages;

- avoid messages building up in your Inbox;

- keep only those messages that you need to keep;

- store your messages in a way that makes it easy for you to work with them.

Also, you should make arrangements so that your Inbox is dealt with if you are likely to be away for some time, for example, if you are on holiday. You may be able to do this in a number of ways depending on the facilities of your e-mail system (see also 'using filters and auto-management facilities', p.62.). For example, you may be able to:

- delegate messages to another person so that any incoming messages are automatically sent to them;

- use an auto-response facility to notify the sender that you are away.

❝You should manage your e-mail in-tray (Inbox) in a similar way to your paper in-tray❞

Some e-mail systems allow you to order your messages in a number of ways, for example, by date/time received, by subject or by sender's e-mail address. You can use these facilities to prioritize your Inbox.

Your messages may even have a priority (such as high, medium and low) assigned to them (see 'assigning a priority to a message', p.154).

You may even be able to preview messages. For example, in Microsoft® Outlook® 2000 you can configure your Inbox so that you can preview the first few lines of your messages without having to open them (and therefore not just rely on the subject line). You can then respond to the most important messages first.

"You should review your 'Sent messages' folder periodically (such as weekly) and delete unwanted messages**"**

managing the messages that you have sent

Many e-mail systems keep a copy of the messages that you send (for example, in a 'Sent messages' folder). Unless you delete these messages the folder will grow and grow. You should review your 'Sent messages' folder periodically (such as weekly) and delete unwanted messages.

addresses, address lists and distribution lists

choosing e-mail addresses

For businesses, the choice of e-mail address can be significant and, like your phone number, if you want to change it later, it can be inconvenient for you and all the people that use it.

If your company moves premises you are likely to need to change your business cards, office stationery and your listings in phone and other direc-tories. And, of course, you will need to tell your customers, suppliers and others. However, unlike the postal service, there is no one who will be able to redirect all your e-mail messages. You may have to come to an arrangement with your ISP, if that is possible.

You should think carefully about the e-mail address(es) that you choose. You should consider registering an Internet domain name for your company and using that, regardless of which ISP you sign up with. Therefore if you change your

ISP, your domain name will follow you. There are many companies that can register your domain name; ISPs are a good starting point – see their web sites.

You should always use role names for company functions that are generic. This is because people often leave companies whereas roles are seldom removed. So if you move location or restructure your company the generic e-mail addresses should still be valid.

> **▶▶▶ CASE STUDY** A company takes the time and trouble to obtain a web domain name but on its web site puts down individual e-mail addresses for the contact points, one of whom is the person who will pay the annual renewal fee to the ISP.
>
> After two years, when the renewal notices get sent out by the ISP, the person responsible has since left the company. So the e-mail server rejects the mail message (because the System Administrator is on the ball and knows that old e-mail addresses should be purged to stop the e-mail server filling up with dead mail).
>
> As a result, the renewal fee is not paid and the domain name goes back into the pot. At worst, the company will have lost its investment in creating its web site as well as its e-mail capability. At best, it will have to spend a lot of time and effort in convincing the authorities that it should keep its domain name.
>
> The situation might have been avoided by having a role and allocating that role to specific individuals or groups of individuals.

Some examples of roles that a company could use are:

- *hostmaster* – for domain name queries
- *postmaster* – for e-mail administration
- *webmaster* – for WWW administration and publishing
- *info* or *help* – for company and product information enquiries
- *accounts* – for payments
- *sales* – for doing business
- *marketing* – for publicity and press releases
- *helpdesk* – for general support.

The first four roles are de facto Internet standards for role names. Most regular Internet users would try one of these names if they did not have a specific e-mail address to use.

address lists

An address list (or Address book) acts as a 'contacts' list. For example, Microsoft® Outlook® 2000 allows you to store details about your customers, including their business details such as company name, address, job title, phone number, fax number and web page address.

An address list allows you to look up and organize your e-mail addresses in a form that you choose rather than holding them under the e-mail names, which might bear little relation to the individual's name.

You may be able to share the address book and therefore maintain a core list of business contacts. Always remember that people's e-mail addresses can change and they may not always notify you. Indeed they may not even be aware that you have their address.

Finding someone's e-mail address can be a challenge. Most service providers offer facilities to search for e-mail addresses but this does not necessarily mean that you will be able to find the address that you want. Many companies do not publish their full lists of e-mail addresses for public scrutiny. (On page 164 are some guidelines on finding someone's e-mail address.)

>>> **WATCH POINT** You may want to preserve your address lists when you either change e-mail packages or upgrade your existing package to a new software version.

For example, if you are a sales representative who has built up a long and valuable list of contacts in your e-mail address book, you will want to make sure that this list is preserved when you change your software or move to a new PC.

If you do not preserve the list you may have to re-key the addresses, assuming that you have no other way of getting them. If you do not want to lose your address list, back it up regularly and before any system changes or upgrades. Also, before any system changes or upgrades are made check for the best way to migrate the list.

---

distribution lists

You may be able to set up a list (or group) of addresses under a single name. This can be very useful if, for example, you are the secretary of a meeting and every week you need to send minutes to the same group of people. The facility is less useful if it becomes abused and trivial messages get broadcast around large organizations merely because the originators do not bother to identify the correct addressees.

▶▶▶ WATCH POINT If you broadcast information to all your employees, or a large group of them, make sure it is checked first by someone other than the person who created the message.

If you get something wrong (such as forgetting to attach a file) you may get a response from each person. If you sent the message to 1,000 people, for example, prepare yourself for the onslaught of messages you are likely to receive. As well as wasting your time, you will be wasting the time of each person who received your message.

In a company using e-mail, each employee will have their own address book that will almost certainly differ from those of other employees. There may be a need to synchronize these lists and some products have better facilities than others to enable this.

As with address lists, if you change e-mail packages or upgrade your existing package to a new software version you may want to preserve your group lists.

working with attachments

Files that are attached to messages usually take up space in addition to that taken up by the message itself. This space can become quite significant. For example, a document created by one leading brand of word processor occupies 19Kb even if it contains only a single word. Hence an apparently small e-mail message with several apparently small attachments might occupy a disproportionate amount of disk space (see also 'attaching files to messages', p.148).

As with address lists, if you change e-mail packages or upgrade your existing package to a new software version you may want to preserve your group lists

If you really want the attachments you should store them outside your e-mail system and then delete them from the e-mail system as soon as possible.

▶▶▶ WATCH POINT

- Be wary of attachments to messages from unknown sources or sources that you cannot trust.

- Attachments are one of the main ways that viruses are spread and they are often spread unknowingly.

- Always use anti-virus software.

- If you are in any doubt about an attachment, do not open it.

▶▶▶ INFO POINT A filter is software that can examine incoming and outgoing messages (including their addresses, subject lines, content and attachments) and takes actions depending upon rules defined to it.

using filters and auto-management facilities
filters

In general, filters can be configured to:

- block messages to or from specific e-mail addresses;

- block messages based on their content (for example, if they contain 'undesirable' words) or size, including the content or size of attachments;

- scan attachments for viruses;

- append disclaimers and confidentiality notices to outbound messages.

Filters can operate at two levels: server level and client level.

▶▶▶ EXAMPLE There is research underway to enable images to be analysed intelligently, for example, to detect pornographic material. Some companies are already checking images attached to e-mail messages for tones which are flesh coloured.

---

server-level filters

These filters are often used to detect inappropriate messages and can incorporate elements which check the content of messages as well as checking for viruses. They can, for example, be configured to scan for swear words or other undesirable content. Messages found to contain suspect material can be rejected or routed to a specific e-mail address for further investigation. Many organizations use these filters to monitor incoming and outgoing messages.

The management of server-level filters is usually carried out centrally within an organization, often by those responsible for the overall management of the system (such as an IT support unit). One good reason for managing these filters centrally is that they can be configured to reflect corporate e-mail policy (see Chapter 6).

client-level filters

Some e-mail clients have a facility that can automatically make decisions about the messages that you receive. In Microsoft® Outlook® you can use the Inbox Assistant to enter criteria (such as the sender's e-mail address or key words in the subject line) which are used to decide whether or not a message should be downloaded. You can also use the same facility to direct downloaded messages to specific folders of your choice, again based on the criteria that you enter. So, for example, you can state that if the subject line contains the phrase 'special offers' you do not want to receive the message. Alternatively, if the message is from OurCompany you can direct it to a folder specifically created for that company.

You can also specify that certain messages are automatically forwarded to a contact in your address book (see also 'auto-management facilities' below).

auto-management facilities

Some e-mail systems provide a facility to respond automatically to messages. For example, Microsoft® Outlook® 2000 has an 'Out of Office Assistant' which you can use to reply automatically to messages when you are unavailable (and in doing so suggest an alternative contact). Similarly, you may be able to redirect (or delegate) messages to another person.

> **"** Some e-mail clients have a facility that can automatically make decisions about the messages that you receive **"**

There are also products available designed to manage messages automatically, including reading, reply to, storing, monitoring and reporting on them. The products may include advanced pattern recognition to categorize incoming messages and direct them to the appropriate department. There are claims of being able to reply accurately to 80 per cent of incoming messages. At least one product vendor suggests that their auto-responding software can even identify the attitude of the sender. Auto-responding software is most commonly used in larger organizations and it operates at the server level.

❝ There is no doubt that spam is annoying❞

managing spam

A search of over 700 published e-mail articles revealed that 65 per cent of them referred to 'spam'. There is no doubt that spam is annoying.

Spammers obtain e-mail addresses through a variety of mechanisms. These include:

- Purchasing them from someone who has already collected them. This is by far the easiest way. Selling e-mail lists can be a profitable business.

- Searching through Usenet messages, either manually or using software, to collect e-mail addresses; a number of discussion groups also post their discussions on the web.

- Examining web pages for mail-to entries or items that look like e-mail addresses. This can be done using automated software.

- Examining e-mail directories, again using automated software.

> ➤➤➤ WATCH POINT Be careful about replying to spam.
> Messages have been sent which say: 'If you don't want to receive any future e-mail from us, use the Reply button and place the word cancel in the subject header'. By doing as they suggest, you may be doing little more than confirming your e-mail address and proving that it is active.

Although spam may be inexpensive to the originator there are costs that others may have to bear. For example:

- the computer processing time on each server through which the message passes;
- the bandwidth consumption, which may in turn slow access for others;
- the storage as the message sits in a queue on the ISP's server;
- the cost and time the recipient spends to download the message;
- the time the recipient spends reading the message.

How can you shield your business from spam? Here are some suggestions that may help but bear in mind that determined spammers are always looking for new ways to achieve their aims.

1. Never reply to a spam message.
2. Guard your e-mail address carefully. Consider using different e-mail addresses for business use, surfing the web, personal use, etc.
3. Request the removal of your details from any Internet-wide e-mail directories.
4. Make sure that you do not authorize the publication of your e-mail details when filling in forms.
5. Ask your e-mail System Administrator to block the offending mail site.
6. Configure your mail reader software to ignore obvious spam messages.
7. Report any instances of spam to the e-mail System Administrator responsible for the server. Remember to include all the information about the message.

Furthermore, some concerned Internet users have established a number of organizations that offer pragmatic solutions to managing spam. One example is the Open Relay Behaviour-modification System (ORBS) which provides a validated database of e-mail systems that do not block the connection of spammers. ORBS will provide its database to companies and so allow e-mail System Administrators to block any messages originating or relayed from

>>> WATCH POINT

● Your e-mail address is not 'public'.

● Treat e-mail addresses as you would your postal address and phone number.

● Do not give out anyone else's e-mail address without getting their permission.

systems listed in the database. In this way, e-mail from a possible source of spam can be stopped.

Most ISPs now have entries in their Terms and Conditions that prohibit the sending of spam by subscribers. Anyone found breaching these conditions is likely to have their service revoked.

" Communicating with a mobile workforce or having staff who are often moving between offices or locations can be an administrative nightmare – and not just for e-mail **"**

managing messages on the move

Communicating with a mobile workforce or having staff who are often moving between offices or locations can be an administrative nightmare – and not just for e-mail. Here are some of the points that mobile users will need to address.

1. Make sure that the device (laptop, PDA, etc.) has adequate security to stop unauthorized access to it. This should ensure that any private messages remain private.

2. Synchronizing message folders between the mobile device, an office-based PC and the e-mail server. This will often involve the use of a protocol such as IMAP4, where messages are held on the server and only copies held on the office-based and mobile devices.

3. Make sure that any mechanisms provided to allow remote access to the e-mail server are secure.

4. Follow the guidelines given by your organization – if they exist. Many large corporations have standards regarding the use of e-mail over remote connections. Many organizations actually forbid such connections.

However, managing mobile communications can involve a number of complex issues. If you are in any doubt about the issues involved, or how to address them, you should get professional advice.

working off-line

If your company does not have a private network or dedicated communication line, you can work off-line and only connect to your ISP when you send and receive messages.

Working off-line can reduce your connection costs and free up your phone line. Most e-mail packages give you the option to work both 'on-line' and 'off-line'.

If you subscribe to a Newsgroup you can download news messages, disconnect and then read the messages.

The most natural way for a full-time employee with a fixed desk to work is 'on-line', but this is not always the most convenient way or the most cost effective. For example you may wish to read your messages from your lap-top computer while travelling home on the train or you may wish to send messages from your home or from one of your branch offices.

Typically your 'mailbox' – which is the folder into which the central e-mail system will place your incoming mail – will be located on a central server. This is readily accessible while you are working on-line. Additionally, there is usually an option to have your messages copied into a local mailbox on your own hard drive so that they may still be accessed while your computer is disconnected from the network (for example, while you are travelling on the train).

Any messages that you create while working off-line will be stored in a local file and when you next connect to the network these messages will be sent to their recipients.

Although these processes are largely automatic, depending on the actual package you are using, they may require some small manual intervention. You must take care to manage these procedures correctly otherwise there is a danger that messages that you may think have been sent only get as far as the temporary storage on your own machine. Checking the status of messages in your Outbox usually reveals whether or not they have been truly sent.

Working off-line can be very useful as it not only frees you from the need for a physical network connection, but also from the network charges while you are disconnected. However, it can introduce complexities as you may end up with both a duplicated mailbox and a duplicated diary. If you have a diary that

❝ Working off-line can reduce your connection costs and free up your phone line ❞

is subject to last-minute changes you will still need to check your 'master' diary on the network to confirm that details of your important meetings have remained unchanged while you have been off-line.

rules of good e-mail management

➤➤➤ HOT TIP 'Managing e-mails is not about the application of science; it's about the application of common sense.'

Peter Howes
Director, @rchive-it.com

There are certain activities that you should carry out regularly on your e-mail system. How often you perform them will not necessarily be the same for all activities and may be influenced by the environment in which you work. Many companies have defined formal procedures for these activities. These activities are summarized below in the form of a set of rules.

1. **Read all of your new e-mail messages at least once in every 24-hour period.**

   However, unless your job really requires it, do not sit in front of the screen waiting for messages. In some offices it is the practice to clear incoming mail first thing every morning and then again immediately after lunch.

2. **Do not let messages build up in your Inbox.**

   You will not be able to see the new e-mails immediately and, even worse, important priority messages might well be hidden among the old, already handled messages.

3. **Reply to messages as soon as you can.**

   Aim to reply to messages within a reasonable time, say within two working days.

4. **Delete messages as soon as you no longer need them.**

   On many e-mail systems, when you delete messages they are moved to a 'Deleted items' folder. You may then have to delete items from this folder. You can configure some systems automatically to empty the contents of a 'Deleted items' folder.

5. **Open your 'Sent messages' folder at least once a week and delete old messages that you no longer need.**

   Your 'Sent messages' folder can build up quickly and you may not always need to keep copies of the messages that you send.

6. **Set an auto-reply, if your mail system has the feature, when you are likely to be out of the office for some time, for example, if you are on holiday.**

   This will give the sender the opportunity to contact another person in your absence if the need arises. Alternatively, some systems allow you to delegate your e-mail to another user.

7. **Keep your address book up-to-date.**

   Like the postal service, undeliverable e-mail is often ignored and you may be given no notification that your message has not been delivered.

8. **Back up important messages and protect them if necessary.**

   Keep a copy of important messages and archive those that you may need in the longer term but not in the shorter term. Protect messages that contain important information. When you back up or archive messages, think about how you will retrieve them.

9. **Change your password at least once a month and do not give anyone else your e-mail password.**

   This makes good sense whatever system you are using.

10. **Use a virus checker and keep it up to date.**

    Viruses are often spread unintentionally. You should check all attachments for viruses, even if you know the sender. Ideally you should configure your system so that all attachments are checked automatically for viruses. Also, as soon as a new virus is created your virus checker may be out of date, so update regularly.

summary

The general principles of good information management apply to e-mail as they do to other media:

- You should keep what you need to keep and only what you need to keep.

- You should keep it in a way that makes it easy to find.

- You should protect it if it is important.

But managing e-mail means more than just managing your e-mail messages. For example, you should choose your e-mail addresses wisely and maintain your address lists. You should also consider the level of service that you get from your service provider and ensure that it is sufficient for your needs.

Over time many of us have idiosyncrasies in the way that we operate and we develop a way of doing things that works for us. There is no single way of managing e-mail that works for everyone, but there are a number of facilities that most e-mail systems have which can help us.

There are a number of rules that you should apply to manage your e-mail effectively, but perhaps the most important rule is to apply common sense.

e-mail and security

> **at a glance**

the need for security

elements of security

encryption

attachments

operational considerations

choosing a secure e-mail product

security in practice

summary

the need for security

why secure e-mail?

Security of communications is not a new problem. Letters get lost in the post and get wrongly delivered. They can also be opened illegally by people if they think the contents may be of value, or perhaps they may be just curious. And of course letters can be forged.

Phone numbers get dialled incorrectly and crossed lines do happen. If there are other people in the room when you make a call, they might be able to hear what you say.

E-mail systems suffer from similar problems. Messages get lost. They can be sent to the wrong address or intercepted in transit. Messages can be forged.

>>> **WATCH POINT** Looking at the Internet from a security angle:

● no one is in control

● there is a variety of e-mail client software but security features are not always compatible

● System Administrators may have access to your messages.

You might not even be able to identify the sender of a message that you receive. If someone wants to hide their identity they can send their messages via an 'anonymous re-mailer'.

>>> **INFO POINT** Anonymous re-mailing is a service offered by a small number of Internet sites. When they receive a message, they remove the identity of the sender, insert an alias (which is randomly generated) and forward the message to the intended recipient.

Furthermore, the flexibility of being able to attach files to messages means that it is also possible to embed viruses in those attachments, either intentionally or unintentionally.

However, the security of e-mail systems is developing rapidly and there are several ways of protecting messages and the information contained within them.

categorizing information to be protected

You should consider what information you need to protect and make sure you protect it appropriately. Protecting messages and attachments to messages, for example by encrypting them, requires some effort, however small, by you and the recipient and you both need to have the appropriate security software.

But if the information is not important then why bother protecting it in an e-mail message? Why, for example, would you need to protect a message to a customer in which you are attaching a product price list that is freely available in the public domain?

Many companies categorize their information and specify how each category should be treated. For example:

- *Operational risk*: information which would cause serious damage to the company if it was disclosed; for example, the secret ingredient of the company's primary product.

- *Reputational risk*: information which would be embarrassing to the company if it was disclosed; for example, details of a customer's orders.

- *No risk*: public information; for example, product catalogues.

Some people suggest four or even five categories, but these can be complicated to administer. Alternatively, you could simplify matters and have only two categories:

- *Risk*: protect it.
  You can then decide on the level of protection.

- *No risk*: do not protect it.

However, you may already categorize information and therefore you may decide to continue to use those categories.

" You should consider what information you need to protect and make sure you protect it appropriately **"**

elements of security

basic security needs

The security of e-mail is often summarized by the letters CIA.

- *Confidentiality*: ensuring that the contents of messages are not disclosed to third parties.

- *Integrity*: ensuring that messages reach the intended recipient and the contents of the messages have not become altered, accidentally or deliberately, during transmission.

- *Authentication*: ensuring that the messages really have come from those who appear to have sent them and that the sender cannot later deny having sent them (sometimes referred to as non-repudiation).

However, there are other aspects of security that must also be addressed. They should be considered for all computer systems and are relevant to e-mail. They include:

- *Viruses*: ensuring that systems are not infected by viruses contained in incoming and outgoing messages.

- *Unauthorized access*: ensuring that systems are 'closed' to those who do not have permission to access them.

- *System attacks*: ensuring that systems are protected from deliberate attacks intended to damage or disrupt your business.

All these aspects are discussed in this chapter.

> ►►► HOT TIP You should look at the possible risks, assess their impact on your business and then implement suitable security to protect yourself against those risks, according to their importance.
>
> Integralis Network Systems Ltd

confidentiality

keeping things secret

There may be significant consequences if someone other than the intended recipient can read the content of your messages.

>>> **EXAMPLE** In World War II the fact that British intelligence could read highly confidential German messages had a major effect on shortening the war.

Today, if a business competitor is able to access and read confidential messages about your business plans then he could soon defeat you in the marketplace.

>>> **INFO POINT** Who can read your messages?
When a message is sent it passes through many servers before it reaches its destination. Each server should have an Administrator and they may be allowed legitimately to view the messages that pass through their server – for example to detect unlawful material.

While the basic risks are the same for e-mail as for any other type of communication, there are some differences.

- E-mail is a digital medium so it is very easy to change parts of the text without leaving any obvious trace. Without any additional help, the recipient would find it very difficult to know if a message had been tampered with.

- It may not be possible to detect if a message has been read while it has been in transit. With Internet mail, you have no control over how your message is delivered. It is quite possible that if you send a message from London to Paris it will go via Chicago, for example.

However, although the technology of e-mail has increased some of these risks, it has also provided methods of controlling them. You can keep messages confidential by encrypting them (see 'encryption', p.82).

integrity

assured delivery

If you are sending something of value through the post you want to be sure it is delivered to the correct address. The risk is that somebody may intercept the post and remove the item of value. When you send an object of value you might

❝You can keep messages confidential by encrypting them❞

protect yourself against this risk by sending it as registered mail – in which case the passage of the letter is tracked through the system, right up to when the recipient has signed for it. If it does go missing you can find out where and when it was intercepted. The same would hold true if the letter contained some intangible item of value, such as an invitation to a party. In this case the assured delivery has to be within a given time – a party invitation is of no value once the party is over.

▶▶▶ WATCH POINT There are no guarantees on delivery of Internet e-mail. Most of the time it works quickly and efficiently, but it is all done on a 'best endeavour' basis. When things go wrong there may not be anyone there to fix it.

At present there is no widespread method to assure the delivery of e-mail messages. Some e-mail systems enable you to request an 'acknowledgement of receipt' (see p.155). However, although this can be a useful facility, it is not available to all e-mail systems. Also, to be able to rely on the acknowledgement, the acknowledgement would need to be digitally signed (see 'digital signatures and certificates', p.83).

66 You can ensure the integrity of messages by using digital signatures 99

correct content

Even when a message appears to have been delivered correctly, the recipient may still want to confirm that the text of the message has not been tampered with either accidentally or deliberately. Concerns about the accuracy of messages go back to the start of communications and there have been numerous court cases relating to them.

▶▶▶ **CASE STUDY** In the early days of the electric telegraph, a gun dealer in the USA telegraphed a message to a potential buyer saying: 'I have thirty rifles to sell at $10 each.' The buyer wanted to buy 3 (three) rifles and telegraphed 'I will buy th[re]e rifles.' But the message got corrupted, 'three rifles' became 'the rifles', and the dealer dispatched all thirty rifles. The US court ruled that the buyer had contracted to buy all thirty.

You can ensure the integrity of messages by using digital signatures.

authentication

authenticating the sender

When you receive a letter through the post, there are usually a few clues that help you confirm who actually sent it. The postmark will tell you whereabouts the letter was posted; it may be written on company stationery; you may recognize the handwriting or the signature. Usually there is enough information to be sure the letter did actually come from the person you thought it did. But in some cases this may not be enough.

> ➤➤➤ **EXAMPLE** In the US navy a submarine captain needs to be totally sure that a message commanding him to launch his nuclear weapons does indeed come from his own commander-in-chief. One solution to this is that the commanding officer gives the captain a secret key at the start of his voyage. The captain then knows that only messages which contain that secret code are authentic – and he assumes, of course, that the key won't get into the wrong hands.

❝ You can authenticate the senders of messages by using digital signatures and certificates❞

With e-mail, to a large extent you are in the hands of the senders. You may have to agree in advance how you will authenticate each other. You can authenticate the senders of messages by using digital signatures and certificates (see 'digital signatures and certificates', p.83).

Without the help of digital signatures and certificates there is no straightforward way to be sure that the sender is the person they purport to be. Nevertheless, some simple checks are worthwhile. For example, before opening a message you might ask the question: does this person usually send me messages? If you are not sure about the sender of a messages that you receive, then be very wary of opening any attachment as it could contain a virus.

viruses

threat of viruses

Even if you can ensure confidentiality and integrity and authenticate the sender of a message, the message could still contain a virus. Neither the sender nor receiver may know it until it is too late. The problem of viruses is a very real one.

>>> INFO POINT

● There are over 13,000 known viruses and potentially many more unknown and in the wild which have not been identified and have no known protection or cure.

● Approximately 100 new viruses are identified every day.

● Over 50 per cent of UK organizations have suffered some kind of security breach or virus intrusion in the past 12 months.

● According to the National Computer Centre (NCC), the cost to UK businesses is estimated at nearly £2bn each year.

Source: IT Network Journal

>>> **EXAMPLE** A UK bank automatically scans about 30,000 Internet messages each day for viruses. The scanning reveals between 30 and 60 (that is 0.1 per cent and 0.2 per cent) messages which are treated as potentially containing a virus and therefore needing further investigation.

❝For e-mail users, the main threat of viruses comes from attachments to messages❞

There are two main types of virus:

1. *Program viruses*   these attach to a program when the programs runs. They also include 'boot sector' viruses which run when you switch on the computer.

2. *Macro viruses*   these are contained in data files for applications such as word processors or spreadsheets.

Viruses can be either malicious or non-malicious. Program viruses can be extremely damaging, for example, deleting all the files on your PC's hard drive as soon as you run the program that the virus has infected. Macro viruses have tended to be an annoyance rather than damaging, but recently they have become more dangerous.

For e-mail users, the main threat of viruses comes from attachments to messages. Once you select an attachment to a message you may start running a new application, quite separate from the e-mail system, to 'open' the attached file. The issue is how can you be sure that that 'foreign' application will be well behaved and not corrupt your system. The usual method is to employ a virus checking utility – that is, software that can check individual files (or even whole computer disks) for viruses. However, there is a continual battle as the virus writers try to produce ever more sophisticated viruses that will not be detected and the virus checkers develop ever more powerful checking tools.

There is a new type of virus surfacing which does not appear in the form of an attachment. The virus is embedded in HTML – formatted messages as software (such as a Visual Basic Script); the act of viewing the e-mail message can activate the virus. An example of this type of virus is the Bubbleboy virus (which, at the time of writing, had not appeared in the wild).

protection against infection

Protection against viruses takes two main forms:

1. *Anti-virus software*: Anti-virus software can be placed on client machines and is usually configured so that it checks files (such as attachments to e-mail messages) automatically when they are opened. There are several well-known software packages on the market.

    Also, network level virus checkers can be configured automatically to scan incoming and outgoing messages for viruses. Messages that are found to contain a virus (or possible virus) can be rejected or routed to a specific e-mail address for further investigation.

2. *Policy and procedures*: To minimize the risk of being infected by a virus you will need to be vigilant and keep to a rigid anti-virus policy. Some of the key points of such a policy are:

    - *'belt and braces'*: check for viruses at all main points of attack: entry points into the system, storage areas (such as file servers and post offices) and when you open the attachment.
    - *up to date*: make sure that all anti-virus software is kept up to date. Most vendors will provide regular monthly or quarterly updates to check for the latest viruses, together with a 'hot fix' for rapid upgrades to protect against any particularly virulent virus.
    - *awareness*: always be alert to the potential risk of viruses. Most viruses will be activated only when the file attached to the message is opened. If you

❝To minimize the risk of being infected by a virus you will need to be vigilant and keep to a rigid anti-virus policy❞

receive a file attachment from an unknown source then consider deleting the file and ignoring the message rather than risk getting a virus. You could also ask the sender to re-send the file as plain text (see 'text format', p.147).

You should also remind your staff regularly about the possible risks and impact of viruses and give them appropriate guidance. Although protection from viruses usually focuses on checking incoming messages, you should also take steps to make sure that the messages you send do not contain viruses.

❝ You should also remind your staff regularly about the possible risks and impact of viruses and give them appropriate guidance❞

> **▶▶▶ EXAMPLE** A prominent Japanese bank inadvertently sent an e-mail message containing a virus to a number of its business associates. On a particular day of the month the virus would trigger a screen message containing an insulting remark.

unauthorized access

People may want to access your e-mail system for legitimate reasons (such as your staff, to send and receive business messages) and illegitimate reasons (such as hackers, to cause disruption to your business). There are a number of ways to control access to your systems.

userid and password control

For users on a network or with shared access to an e-mail system, a UserId and password should be used to control access.

Although the administration of UserIds and passwords falls mainly in the domain of Systems Administrators rather than individual users, there are several steps that you can take as an end user. The steps apply equally to any assigned UserId and password, and not just for e-mail systems. For example:

● Do not give your password to anyone else.

● Change your password frequently.

● If you leave your machine unattended then you should exit your e-mail system. As a second line of defence, use a 'screen saver' (set to activate after, say, five minutes) and protect it with another password.

Using a UserId and password may help the recipients of your messages because it can be key to assuring that the messages really do come from you.

firewalls

>>> **INFO POINT** A firewall is a combination of hardware and software that acts as a security boundary between parts of a network. Firewalls are often used by companies to provide 'safe' access between their private networks and the public Internet.

Firewalls act at a network level. They can be used to check the address and type (such as SMTP) of incoming messages but they do not consider the content of messages. They can be likened to 'passport control' at a border point. There is a check on the permission to travel but not of the baggage being carried. Checking the message content (baggage) is the responsibility of filters (x-ray machines), the most common form of which is virus checkers.

Companies that use firewalls will usually have a security policy that defines who is able to configure and manage the firewall. This is often the responsibility of a central unit such as an IT support unit.

system attacks

There are other security risks that your company could face such as a deliberate attack on your e-mail system, intended to damage or disrupt your business. For example, corporate e-mail systems can be flooded by messages that eventually use up all available resources and seriously degrade performance and sometimes even crash the systems. Consider what happens when your system receives a message that has an invalid e-mail address which is quite close to a real address. It may well come through your firewall, through your content checker and be sent to one of your post offices before the invalid address is detected. If many such messages are received in quick succession then your server's performance may be degraded.

Direct attacks such as viruses and flooding are targeted to disrupt or destroy the e-mail systems themselves rather than damage individual messages. For this reason protection falls mainly in the domain of Systems Administrators rather than individual users.

Protection against these types of attack may mean having to apply the full range of security measures including firewalls, filters, virus checkers and operational procedures – and these should all be backed up with an effective security policy.

encryption

Encryption addresses the key requirements for 'secure' e-mail messages, namely confidentiality, integrity and authentication. It is based on using 'keys' to encrypt and decrypt messages.

There needs to be a mechanism that allows the genuine recipients to 'unscramble' the information. Hence there must be agreement and collaboration between the senders and the recipients before encryption can be adopted. There is more than one approach to this problem.

>>> **INFO POINT** Encryption is a process that 'scrambles' information so that it can only be unscrambled by someone who has an appropriate de-scrambler (or key).

choice of encryption standards

An advantage of standards in the computer industry is that there are so many to choose from! The only factor that standards in the computer industry seem to have in common is that they use a TLA (three-letter acronym). Encryption standards are no different in this respect – DES, PGP, PKI, RSA, etc. But they do fall into two main types – symmetric and asymmetric.

symmetric encryption

In symmetric encryption both the sender and receiver share the same secret key, and that same key is used to encrypt and decrypt messages. This type of system is comparatively fast and is ideal for closed user groups (such as a company's internal network) where a System Administrator can distribute the keys to all the individuals. An example of this type of system is the Data Encryption Standard (DES), also known as the Data Encryption Algorithm (DEA).

>>> **INFO POINT** The Data Encryption Standard (DES) is the most widely used data encryption standard – banks use it to secure the transfer of funds electronically.

It was developed by IBM and adopted as a standard by the US National Bureau of Standards in 1977. However, in 1986 the US National Security Agency stated that it would stop certifying DES. Nevertheless, it still remains the most popular standard.

For example, using DES with a 56-bit key generates 72,000,000,000,000,000 (that is, 7.2×10^{16}) key combinations.

asymmetric encryption

In asymmetric encryption each user has a pair of keys – a public key and a private key. The public key is freely available and is used to encrypt messages. The private key is known only to the recipient and is used to decrypt the message. The mathematics is such that although the public key can be used to encrypt a message, only the private key can be used to decrypt it.

This type of system is slower than DES but provides a solution to the problem of open systems (such as the Internet) where each user can distribute their public key to anyone with whom they want to communicate. An example of this type of system is Public Key Infrastructure (PKI, see p.85).

There are now a number of products working to a combined approach using PKI to establish a secure communication between sender and recipient, and then using that connection to exchange a symmetric DES key for the actual message.

digital signatures and certificates

In the same way that a handwritten signature on a printed document provides some degree of confirmation that it originated from a particular person, a digital signature provides similar confirmation of the origins of an electronic document.

However, the technology used to implement a digital signature provides a far higher degree of security than a handwritten signature. It is possible to verify that the message was created by the person signing it and that the message has not been altered since it was signed. Digital signature systems also

**❝ Digital
signatures
enable the
recipient of a
digital
message to be
assured of
both the
identity of the
sender and the
integrity of the
message❞**

allow for non-repudiation of the signed message: that is, the sender cannot later deny sending the message by claiming that the signature was forged.

Digital signatures enable the recipient of a digital message to be assured of both the identity of the sender and the integrity of the message. The technology used to implement digital signatures is the same as that used to encrypt data: that is, public key encryption. This technology provides two keys – one is public and is made public and the other is private to the individual (and must be kept so). The combination of a public key, private key and digital signature is sometimes referred to as a 'digital ID'.

The technology also makes use of digital certificates. These are software 'tokens' provided by trusted third parties, called Certification Authorities (CAs), who will vouch for the identity of the person or organization for which they were issued. A digital certificate includes details of any public keys issued to the certificate holder.

A number of packages are available that make use of digital certificates and public/private keys to ensure that messages are both digitally signed and/or encrypted. Perhaps the most wellknown of these is PGP® (Pretty Good Privacy) which is available as both freeware downloadable from the Internet and as a commercial product from Network Associates. This software will integrate with the main varieties of e-mail client software, for example, Microsoft® Outlook®, to provide a full range of very powerful encryption facilities.

If you want to get someone's digital certificate so that you can send them secure e-mail there are two main options:

- You can search one of the certification authorities' databases (usually available from their web site).

- You can ask the intended recipient to send you a digitally signed message (which will then contain their public key).

▶▶▶ WATCH POINTS

- Look after your private keys.

- Do not give your private key to anyone else.

- Always keep your private key private and do not leave it in your PC in a way that others would be able to use it.

- Remember that this is part of your electronic identity on the Internet and without it you become anonymous and untrustworthy.

public key infrastructure

Public Key Infrastructure (PKI) is a collection of components which provides a secure method of communication. These components include:

"Public Key Infrastructure (PKI) is a collection of components which provides a secure method of communication"

- *an encryption method (or algorithm)*: using keys to encrypt and decrypt messages;

- *digital certificates (keys)*: certifying that the corresponding private key is known only to the individual named on the certificate;

- *digital signatures*: using the certificate to 'sign' messages to show that they are genuine and have not been altered;

- *a mechanism to publish certificates*: a means by which certificates can be issued;

- *trusted third parties*: organizations that can act as trusted third parties to issue certificates.

> **▶▶▶ INFO POINT** The whole of PKI is based on the fact that while it is relatively easy to multiply two prime numbers together it is much harder to factorize the result to get back the original two numbers. The larger the numbers, the harder it is; by the time you get to 10- or 20-digit numbers it is almost impossible.

Although you can use a secure e-mail product without understanding the detailed cryptography underlying the system, some basic knowledge may help to select appropriate products. A more detailed description of PKI is included in Appendix B, p.166.

attachments

This section on attachments is included as a section in its own right to emphasize the fact that if you attach files to messages then you must also consider the security of those files.

In the same way that you can secure messages using encryption and digital certificates, you can also secure attachments. Some applications enable you to encrypt files that you created using those applications. For example, in

Microsoft® Word® you can password protect documents: that is, you can apply a password to a document when you save it so that it can only be opened using the password. You can then use another method (such as the phone) to give the password to the person you want to receive the information.

➤➤➤ **WARNING** If you protect a Microsoft® Word® file with a password and then forget the password, you will not be able to open the file, access the information in it or remove the password protection.

Therefore, you should keep a list of passwords and their associated files. If you do this, make sure you keep the list confidential and that you store it in a safe place.

If you want to secure the contents of an e-mail message, one option is to put the information in an attachment (such as a Microsoft® Word® file) and protect the file with a password. This approach might be appropriate if you or the recipient of your message was not able to use PKI – for example, if your e-mail system does not support encryption – but you can exchange Microsoft® Word® documents.

operational considerations
basic procedures

❝ Good security requires good procedures far more than it requires good technology ❞

Good security requires good procedures far more than it requires good technology.

The encryption technology of the German Enigma machine (the coding machine used by the German High Command in World War II) was superb, but the Allies were able to crack the code because the operators of the machine did not always follow the proper procedures. In one case an operator failed to re-set the machine when re-sending a long message; the code breakers intercepted both messages, realized what had happened and were able to compare them and thus obtained the code settings for that day.

Sending secure messages may not need such elaborate procedures as the Enigma operators, but you do need some operational procedures to make sure that you maintain the integrity of the system. These procedures should be part of your overall security framework. Here are some of the procedures that you should adopt. They relate to sending, receiving and managing messages.

1. **Agree what information needs to be secure.**

   If you make a business decision that, say, your customer list is classified information, then it should be protected everywhere it occurs, not just if it is part of an e-mail message.

   Do not use a security system to send a document if an attacker may already have access to a clear text version of the document. It is then just some extra ammunition to help crack the codes.

   You need clear guidelines to say what information should be encrypted.

2. **Agree what encryption methods will be used.**

   You want to be sure that the recipient will be able to read the message. Therefore you may need to check that the recipient has the right tools to decrypt your message.

3. **Establish processes for the safe management, storage and disposal of confidential messages.**

   If you are sending an encrypted document, you want to be sure that the recipient does not decrypt the message, store it (unencrypted) on their laptop and leave the laptop unprotected.

> ►►► **HOT TIP** The security will only be as good as the weakest link.
> *Integralis Network Systems Ltd*

additional procedures

There are a number of additional security-related procedures that you should consider.

archiving

For statutory or regulatory reasons you may be required to store information safely for a specific length of time. Even though there are no legal requirements for your company to archive its messages, if those archives do exist then the courts can demand access to them. Since the text of messages is stored on servers and the data on those servers is usually backed up, then the chances are that any messages you have written will be backed up, even if you have already deleted them from your computer.

❝For statutory or regulatory reasons you may be required to store information safely for a specific length of time❞

encryption

If a business has set up an e-mail encryption system, then the company security policy must say who is authorized to access encrypted company messages and under what conditions they can do so.

The e-mail system will have been set up for business use, rather than personal use. So although the company may have issued encryption keys to its staff, the company should maintain control over those keys.

authentication

&& The control of authentication keys should lie fully with the member of staff 99

The control of authentication keys should lie fully with the member of staff. If a company had control over the authentication keys of its entire staff, then any member would be able to deny their digital signature on the basis that another company official could have issued it. It is for this reason that two keys are used, one for encryption and one for authentication.

virus checking

There is another twist to e-mail security with the issue of virus checking of encrypted messages. Virus checking software needs to access the text of a message and its attachments.

A corporate virus checking system would need to be able to decrypt all incoming messages, check them for viruses and then re-encrypt them before delivering them to the recipient. So the virus checker needs to hold all the private keys of all the staff in the company, which makes it an obvious target for attack.

A solution may be to perform virus checking of encrypted massages on the recipient's system and back this up with procedures to ensure that the user's system does indeed perform the virus checking.

choosing a secure e-mail product

Once you have decided that you need some additional security for your messages, the next step is to choose a suitable, secure e-mail product. The following is a brief checklist of the main features that you need to consider. The relative importance of each feature will depend on your needs and the needs of your company. The most important features are listed first.

1. *Standards*. The system should use recognized standards that have a wide acceptance. At the time of writing the most widely accepted standard is S-MIME.

2. *Legal acceptability*. Not all countries accept the same level of security. For example, at the time of writing, the use of cryptography was banned in France and Russia and in the USA there was a ban on the export of strong encryption software.

> ➤➤➤ **WATCH POINT** Some vendors might claim that their products are S-MIME compliant. However, do not take their word for it; ask for a demonstration of compatibility.

3. *Usability*. Staff will bypass the security facilities if they are not easy to use.

4. *Functionality*. The product should include these functions:

   - different keys for signing and encryption
   - encryption of message content and attachments
   - secure storage of private keys
   - integration with other desktop applications
   - integration with central directory services.

Putting in place appropriate security can involve a number of complex issues. If you are in any doubt about the issues involved, or how to address them, you should get professional advice.

> **❝Putting in place appropriate security can involve a number of complex issues. If you are in any doubt about the issues involved, or how to address them, you should get professional advice❞**

security in practice

This section contains three case studies that set out realistic, security-related situations for a cross-section of businesses. A brief analysis is followed by possible solutions.

the small business

Each month a small business sends details of its projected sales to one of its suppliers so that the supplier can make sure there is sufficient stock to meet the demand.

analysis

- This is a closed group of users, just two users, so a symmetric key approach is possible.
- The business risk is low so they do not need strong encryption.

solution

- Agree to work with a common spreadsheet application that allows them to password protect files, e.g. Microsoft® Excel®.
- Make contact other than by e-mail, say phone, to agree a shared password.
- Enter the monthly details into the spreadsheet, protect it with the password, save the spreadsheet file and then send the password protected file as an attachment in a standard e-mail message.
- Change the password on a regular basis, say at least every three months, or if they suspect somebody else has discovered the password.

the distributed group

An enthusiastic sole trader is setting up a partnership with a small group of other individuals. They want to exchange details about their business plans without fear of any of their potential competitors finding out.

analysis

- This is an open group of users distributed across the country.
- They will want a low-cost, easy-to-use solution.

solution

- Get basic digital certificates from a mass market supplier such as Verisign.

- Physically exchange public keys, for example, on a floppy disk, when members of the group meet.

- Agree to work with a standard Internet e-mail package, such as Microsoft® Outlook® or Netscape® Communicator® and install the certificates in the e-mail product.

the financial institution

A financial institution wants to allow its customers to send payment instructions via secure e-mail.

analysis

- This will be a large, well-defined group of users, distributed across the country.

- The security requirements will be paramount.

- There is a need for a high degree of trust.

solution

- In the absence of a national or global trust authority, the company will have to set up and administer its own PKI and certificate authority.

- The company should issue certificates only to approved customers on production of some proof of identity.

- The company should provide additional software to support their customers using PKI.

summary

You should consider e-mail security in terms of:

- the information you need to protect;

- the method you use to protect the information;

- the infrastructure that you put in place to manage the security of your e-mail system and the information which passes through it.

The need to secure your e-mail messages is no different to the need to secure any other type of information that you deal with. If the information is important you should secure it; but that does not mean that you need to secure everything.

Although there are numerous standards for encrypting e-mail messages, Public Key Infrastructure (PKI) has emerged as the most dominant.

However, it is not sufficient to have a method for securing the messages that you send. You also need to consider what you do with the secure messages that you receive. Messages and attachments that contain important information should be managed appropriately, and this includes messages which you send, archive or delete.

Security is a two-way street. Even though you may be able to encrypt messages that you send, the recipient may not be able to decrypt them unless they have the appropriate software. Therefore you should think of their capabilities before sending secure messages to them.

Finally, even though you may be able to send and receive secure messages you still need to protect yourself from being infected by or spreading viruses and from other 'attacks' on your system.

e-mail and the law

➤ **at a glance**

general aspects of the law

questions worth asking

key aspects of the law

effective service

e-mail and company stationery

taking legal action

answers to the questions worth asking

summary

general aspects of the law

This chapter has been written with the assistance of David Engel of Theodore Goddard, one of the UK's leading law firms and specialists in 'cyberliability'.

> **▶▶▶ INFO POINT** Theodore Goddard runs The Cyberliability Service, together with network security experts Integralis and insurance brokers Alexander Forbes Risk Services. It provides legal, technical and insurance solutions to the risks of employee access to e-mail and the Internet.
>
> In 1997 Theodore Goddard acted for private medical insurer Western Provident Association (WPA) in the landmark cyberlibel case in the UK when WPA successfully sued rival insurer Norwich Union over defamatory messages circulating on Norwich Union's e-mail systems.

The law has been practised for hundreds of years and much of it relates to communication in the written form. For many years it seemed that any request you made was almost worthless without written confirmation accompanied by a signature, and this paper form was often key evidence in legal proceedings. However, the advances in technology, the advent of the Internet and e-mail bring a fresh set of issues that must be addressed.

As these issues are being addressed, new ones appear. Although the legal profession is working hard to keep pace with them, many of the issues have yet to be 'tested' in the courts.

At the time of writing, e-mail-related case law is very limited so it is not possible to say definitely how the courts will interpret the law for the many situations that will arise.

QA Research conducted independent research during 1998 among a cross-section of 200 UK businesses. The information panels that appear in this chapter are based on that survey.

▶▶▶ **INFO POINT** 57 per cent of UK businesses surveyed were 'concerned' or 'very concerned' about cyberliability.

Any references in this chapter to e-mail messages include attachments to those messages. So, for example, if the law says that you are liable for the contents of a message, then you are also liable for the contents of any attachments to the message.

The content of this chapter is not a complete statement of the law. It does not constitute legal advice and it should not be relied upon as being legal advice.

This chapter highlights many of the key legal issues that you may need to address. Because these issues are important, you should get advice from legal professionals and leave nothing to chance. Many law firms, such as Theodore Goddard, offer specialist services relating to e-mail and the Internet.

> **❝If the law says that you are liable for the contents of a message, then you are also liable for the contents of any attachments to the message❞**

which law applies

One of the characteristics of e-mail (and e-commerce in general) is that it crosses international boundaries as if they were not there and so the laws of more than one country may be appropriate in some cases. If you want to take legal action against someone, depending on the circumstances, you may even be able to choose the country in which you take the action. There is more about this later in the chapter.

Each country has its own law and the law that applies in one particular country may be quite different to the law of another. Even within the same country the law can vary from region to region and so can the interpretation of that law, for example, in the USA.

In order to give some meaningful examples and avoid a text that is too general, this chapter focuses on the law that applies to England and Wales.

"The law is intended to protect everyone and everyone has the right to take action if they think it is appropriate to do so"

who can take action against whom

Actions can be taken by:

- *employers against employees*

  e.g. an employer who discovers that an employee has been sending messages to other employees which contained libellous remarks.

- *employees against employers*

  e.g. an employee who is dismissed after being wrongly accused of sending messages to other employees which contained libellous remarks.

- *third parties against employers and employees*

  e.g. a third party defamed in a libellous message sent by a company employee to a customer.

- *employers and employees against third parties*

  e.g. a company or employee defamed in a message posted on an Internet bulletin board by a third party.

The law is intended to protect everyone and everyone has the right to take action if they think it is appropriate to do so.

questions worth asking

>>> **INFO POINT** 50 per cent of companies have not advised staff of the legal pitfalls associated with e-mail use.

Before exploring the detail of this chapter, ask yourself these questions.

1. Can e-mail messages be used as evidence in a court of law?

2. Should my company e-mail messages contain the same information as that on my company stationery (such as my registered office address and company registration number)?

3. Should I include a disclaimer on all e-mail messages that I send outside my company?

4. Can I confirm a contract with a customer by sending them an e-mail message?

5. If a customer sends me confidential information by e-mail is there anything that would prevent me from forwarding it to other people?

6. As an employer, am I liable if, for example, an employee is downloading from the Internet pornographic material that he/she is then forwarding around the office by e-mail?

7. As an employer, can I hold an employee responsible for any action that may result from something the employee puts in a message?

8. As an employer, am I entitled to look at my employees' e-mail messages?

9. As an employer, could I be liable if an employee sends a message containing a virus to a third party?

10. Can I serve legal documents by e-mail?

11. Is it unlawful to send an e-mail using someone else's e-mail address?

12. If I forward an e-mail message that contains libellous allegations, can action be taken against me?

13. If I receive an e-mail message can I copy part of it and use it in other material?

14. If I receive a libellous (or other offensive) message from someone who is in another country, and I want to take action against them, which law applies – the law of their country or the law of mine?

This chapter answers these questions, but in case you do not have the time to read the chapter, the answers are given on p.112.

key aspects of the law

There are many aspects of the law relating to e-mail that you must consider and those which are key are listed here:

- defamation
- breach of confidence
- sexual and racial harassment
- copyright infringement
- publication of obscene material
- inadvertent formation of contracts
- negligent mis-statement
- data protection obligations
- computer misuse
- negligent virus transmission
- disclosure in legal proceedings
- privacy.

ff Defamation, breach of confidence and sexual and racial harassment are the most prominent in terms of the likelihood of occurrence JJ

Each of these aspects is discussed in the following sections. Defamation, breach of confidence and sexual and racial harassment are the most prominent in terms of the likelihood of occurrence and therefore receive greater focus in this chapter.

defamation

Defamation is an attack on the good reputation of a person or a company. It is applicable to e-mail just as it is to more traditional forms of communication.

Defamation includes both libel and slander. Slander is the communication of an untrue and defamatory statement of fact about a person or a company in an impermanent form, for example, orally. Libel is the communication of such a statement in permanent form and therefore almost certainly includes e-mail – although this point has not yet been tested in the courts in the UK.

> **➤➤➤ INFO POINT** 52 per cent of companies consider that they may be exposed to liability for e-mail libel.

libel

Generally speaking, an untrue statement of fact that damages the reputation of a person or a company or holds them up to hatred, ridicule or contempt is libellous. However, the material need not be obviously insulting. It could, for example, be a suggestion that a competitor is in financial difficulties or unprofessional in the conduct of its business.

In order to prove libel in the UK, three criteria need to be met:

1. There must be the existence of a defamatory statement – that is, one which is likely to make ordinary people think worse of the person or company.

2. It must identify the person or company concerned – that is, would a reasonable person think that the words referred to the person or company?

3. The statement must be 'published' (that is, communicated) to a third party – for example, transmitted by e-mail.

If a libel action does arise, the person or company defamed does not need to prove that damage has occurred to them – this is automatically assumed. Generally speaking, a jury will assess the amount of compensation to award.

who is liable for a libellous statement?

A libel action can be brought against:

- the author of the e-mail;

- the 'publisher' of the e-mail (for example, the author's employer, service provider or access provider).

The author of a libellous message sent by e-mail is responsible for it and will be liable for any damage that it causes to the reputation of the person or company concerned. The author's employer may also be liable for the author's actions if the author is employed under a contract of employment and the actions are committed in the course of their employment – this is known as the principle of vicarious liability.

If a libellous message is forwarded to another person, then the 'forwarder' may also be liable as well as the original author of the message.

> **❝** If a libellous message is forwarded to another person, then the 'forwarder' may also be liable as well as the original author of the message **❞**

In some instances an employer may be able to avoid vicarious liability for the actions of its employees by, for example, demonstrating that the employee was acting outside the scope of his or her employment in sending a libellous e-mail. However, the author's employer may still be liable for a libellous message because, in providing the hardware and the link to the Internet, the employer may be deemed to be a 'publisher'.

In any event, the person or company libelled will be aware that a company is likely to have more money and assets than the author of the libellous material. The person or company defamed may therefore seek to take action against the author's employer rather than the author.

defences to an action in libel

There are two main defences to a libel action:

- justification (that is, truth);
- fair comment on a matter of public interest.

No matter how libellous you have been about a person or a company, if your statements of fact are true, you may be able to rely upon the defence of 'justification'.

❝ You would need to be able to prove that your allegations were true with evidence which is admissible in a court – and e-mail messages can be used as such evidence❞

You would need to be able to prove that your allegations were true with evidence which is admissible in a court – and e-mail messages can be used as such evidence.

Alternatively, if what you said was an expression of opinion rather than a statement of fact, the defence of 'fair comment' may be applicable provided that your comments were on a matter of public interest and were based on true facts of which the reader was aware.

However, more importantly for employers, under the Defamation Act 1996 relief may be at hand for companies who are sued as a 'publisher' of the libellous material, in the shape of a new defence of 'innocent dissemination'. A company may rely on the defence of 'innocent dissemination' provided that:

- the company was not the author, editor or commercial publisher of the statement complained of;
- the company took 'reasonable care' in relation to the publication;

- the company did not know, and had no reason to believe, that what it did caused or contributed to the publication of a defamatory statement.

In deciding the last two points the Act indicates that three factors should be considered:

- the extent of the company's responsibility for the content of the statement or the decision to publish it;

- the nature or circumstances of the publication;

- the previous conduct or character of the author, editor or publisher.

The Act states that a person is not the author, editor or publisher of a statement if he is 'only involved in processing, making copies of, distributing or selling any electronic medium in or on which the statement is recorded or in operating any equipment by means of which the statement is retrieved, copied or distributed' or 'the operator of a communications system by means of which a defamatory statement is transmitted, or made available, by a person over whom he has no effective control'. This defence has yet to be fully tested in the UK courts.

By contrast, in the USA, an employer in the position of a secondary publisher (that is, someone who is unwittingly involved in the dissemination of the defamatory material) would only be liable if the person making the claim could prove that the employer was at fault by allowing the material to be published.

where to sue?

The defamed person or company may sue in any jurisdiction where the libel is 'published' and in which their reputation has been damaged – that is likely to mean any country from which the material may be accessed, not just where the e-mail was sent from. The person or company can 'forum shop' and decide where it is more advantageous for them to sue.

For example, the UK is known for its claimant-friendly libel laws so they may wish to take advantage of these and sue in the UK. Alternatively, the US courts are known for their awards of multimillion dollar damages so they may choose to sue in the USA.

> **❝The defamed person or company may sue in any jurisdiction where the libel is 'published' and in which their reputation has been damaged❞**

breach of confidence

duty of confidence

UK law protects certain types of information from disclosure. The basic principle is that if confidential information is communicated in circumstances which impose a 'duty of confidence' on the recipient, the recipient may not without consent disclose that information to the detriment of the person who is communicating it.

Consider, for example, an employee who is leaving a company to join a competitor. Before leaving he or she forwards a message to their new employer and includes a list of the existing employer's customers and the prices charged for their services. There would be a breach of confidence and the existing employer could take action against the employee.

However, information that is fully available to the public is not protected, even if the initial disclosure was made in breach of confidence.

> ➤➤➤ **WARNING** If information that is confidential to your company were inadvertently made available to a third party, you would lose the benefit of the protection of confidentiality.

Because of the ease with which e-mails can be automatically forwarded and copied, an inadvertent breach of confidence is all the more likely to occur. It is therefore important for any company that uses e-mail to take steps to protect its own confidential information and to make sure that it is not liable to a third party for a breach of confidence.

For example, if you send a message to your bank manager saying that you are in financial difficulty and by mistake you address it to a supplier, you lose the protection of confidentiality. However, your position would be stronger if you had included a disclaimer on you message (see 'protecting confidential information' below).

what information is confidential?

> ➤➤➤ **WARNING** Where confidential information is provided to your company in circumstances where you have a duty to keep it confidential, and that information is then provided to a third party who makes unauthorized use of it, your company may be liable for breach of confidence.

Confidential information may include:

- trade secrets (including software, hardware specifications, company payroll, etc.);

- 'relative secrecy' (such as information widely known to your own company but not to the general public);

- compilations (such as marketing databases which have been compiled using information gathered about customers);
- ideas;
- personal information.

protecting confidential information

To protect confidential information, there are a number of practical steps that you can take, including:

- encrypting the information before you send it (see 'security in practice', p.89);
- raising awareness of the issue among your staff and providing appropriate training (see 'staff education and training', p.130);
- including a suitable confidentiality notice to warn unintended recipients of the confidential nature of the information. This can create grounds for an action for breach of confidence if the information is subsequently misused (see 'disclaimers and confidentiality notices', p.135).

You may already have a policy for protecting this type of information.

liability for breach of confidence

When you, as an employer or employee, receive information in confidence you have a duty not to disclose it without the permission of the person who provided it. There are two defences to a claim for breach of confidence:

> **When you, as an employer or employee, receive information in confidence you have a duty not to disclose it without the permission of the person who provided it**

> **▶▶▶ INFO POINT** 70 per cent of businesses consider that they are exposed to liability for breach of confidence.

- disclosure is in the public interest; and/or
- disclosure will reveal wrongdoing.

sexual and racial harassment

sexual harassment

Sexual harassment means unacceptable conduct of a sexual nature that is:

- unwanted
- unreasonable
- offensive.

In certain circumstances even a single act can constitute harassment. Harassment may be committed by the use of e-mail to send harassing messages to the victim – for example, by making sexual innuendoes. Harassment may also be committed indirectly, by creating a 'hostile workplace' from the victim's perspective, for example, by forwarding sexually explicit images around the office.

>>> INFO POINT 51 per cent of businesses consider themselves exposed to cyberliability for sexual or racial harassment.

If an employee commits an act of sexual harassment, it may result in an action being brought against him or her. The employer is also vicariously liable for the discriminatory acts of its employees and has a duty to protect them from harassment. Furthermore, an employer may also be liable for harassment committed by its contractors if those contractors are within the employer's control.

>>> WARNING Sexual harassment cases are resolved by an industrial tribunal. Such cases often attract significant media interest and could be potentially very damaging to the reputation of your business.

However, an employer may be able to avoid being vicariously liable if it can show that all reasonably practicable steps were taken to prevent the employee from committing the harassment in the course of their employment. The onus is on the employer to show that it attempted to prevent that particular act or that kind of act in general (see 'taking legal action', p.111).

racial harassment

The Race Relations Act 1976 treats racial harassment similarly to the way in which the Sex Discrimination Act 1975 treats sexual harassment. Again, the employer will be vicariously liable for the racial harassment committed by one of its employees where the situation was sufficiently within the employer's control.

Also, the publication of threatening, abusive or insulting material with the intention of stirring up racial hatred is a criminal offence under the Public Order Act 1986.

A statement within your e-mail policy that prohibits sexual and racial harassment is therefore essential, alongside other general warnings and educational activities on the subject of harassment.

copyright infringement

Under the UK's Copyright, Designs and Patents Act 1988, the unauthorized copying of an original work, which includes making a hard or electronic copy (as with e-mails), without the permission of the owner of the copyright of the material, constitutes an infringement of copyright.

The publication of protected material by an employee, for example by posting an e-mail that contains copyright information on a bulletin board, without the permission of the copyright owner, could expose the employee and the company to legal action for copyright infringement. Such an action can include a claim for damages.

Copyright is likely to exist in the following:

- graphics

- music

- computer games

- non-executable material from web sites.

If this material is copied or downloaded where there is no express or implied permission to do so, copyright will be infringed.

> ➤➤➤ **WARNING** The fact that you may not know that your employee has downloaded unlicensed software is not a defence to a copyright infringement action where the downloaded software is being used for work for your company's purpose.

publication of obscene material

The publication of obscene material is a criminal offence. To be obscene, an article needs to be more than just sexually explicit – it must show a tendency to deprave or corrupt. The definition of 'publication' includes transmission of obscene materials – that is, it includes obscene material in or attached to e-mail messages.

❝The publication of obscene material is a criminal offence❞

The publisher's intention is irrelevant. However, it is a defence to prove that the publisher had not examined the article and that it had no reasonable cause to suspect that obscene material of any kind was being distributed using its system.

It is not sufficient for an employer simply to close its eyes to the material held on its system. The employer would only have a defence if it could show that it did not know there was material on its system that was obscene and that this lack of knowledge was not the result of negligence.

inadvertent formation of contracts

➤➤➤ INFO POINT 49 per cent of companies surveyed consider themselves exposed to liability for the inadvertent formation of contractual relations.

Where a third party reasonably believes that an employee of a company has authority to negotiate, or enter into, an agreement on behalf of the company, the employer will be bound by what the employee says. This is known as the rule of 'ostensible authority'.

❝If an e-mail (providing, for example, financial advice) is likely to be identified with the company, the company will be liable for the effect of any advice which the recipient, or even, in some circumstances, a third party reasonably relies upon❞

E-mails are generally identified as originating from a company, so the recipient will in most cases be acting reasonably if they assume that it is sent with the company's authority.

Any contract formed or altered by e-mail may therefore be binding upon the company under the rules of ostensible authority and vicarious liability, even if that employee was not authorized, or was forbidden to enter into such a contract. Therefore, you should consider including in all e-mail messages a suitable disclaimer (see p.135).

negligent misstatement

The law imposes a duty on a person or company to take care when they provide advice to a third party that the third party reasonably relies on; this is known as a 'duty of care'. The same applies to advice provided by e-mail.

➤➤➤ INFO POINT 60 per cent of companies consider themselves exposed to cyberliability for negligent misstatement.

If an e-mail (providing, for example, financial advice) is likely to be identified with the company, the company will be liable for the effect of any advice which the recipient, or even, in some circumstances, a third party, reasonably relies upon. As usual, suitable notices and disclaimers should be used (see p.135).

data protection obligations

(see p.135)

> **➤➤➤ INFO POINT** 60 per cent of UK companies are concerned about cyberliability for breaching their obligations under the Data Protection Act.

It is a criminal offence to collect and process personal data on a computer unless the user of the data is registered with the Data Protection Registrar.[1] It is likely that a significant amount of personal data is sent and received through the e-mail system.

Details of registration should reflect the use of the Internet: for example, the Registrar has recommended that Internet users should register on a 'worldwide' basis.

All data users are required to comply with the Data Protection Principles.

> **➤➤➤ INFO POINT** Data Protection Principles
>
> Personal data must be:
>
> ● obtained, used and processed fairly and lawfully;
>
> ● held only for specifically registered purposes;
>
> ● used and disclosed consistently with those purposes;
>
> ● adequate, relevant and not excessive;
>
> ● kept accurate and up to date;
>
> ● not kept longer than necessary;
>
> ● made available to the individual concerned and to be corrected or erased if justified;
>
> ● kept secure against unauthorized access, loss, disclosure or destruction.

---

[1] At the time of writing the new Data Protection Act 1998 was published but not in force. The new Act refers to a Commissioner, in place of a Registrar.

The Data Protection Principles most likely to be relevant to e-mail use include:

- personal data should be collected and processed fairly and lawfully;
- data should be accurate and kept up to date;
- systems should be secure.

The new Data Protection Act 1998[2] considerably increases the obligations on users of personal data. For example, it includes:

- restrictions on sending personal data to non-European Economic Area (EEA) countries with inadequate protection for data subjects (which may include the USA);
- increased rights of access for the subjects of the data;
- restrictions on the processing of certain 'sensitive data' (such as information about a person's marital status or their ethnic origin).

▶▶▶ INFO POINT 66 per cent of companies considered they were exposed to computer hackers. 14 per cent of companies have had to discipline staff for misuse of e-mail or the Internet at work.

computer misuse

Under the Computer Misuse Act 1990, computer hacking is a criminal offence. Computer hacking includes:

- unauthorized access to a system;
- unauthorized access to a system, with intent to commit further offences;
- unauthorized modification of computer material.

Misuse by an employee of their access to the Internet could result in a criminal prosecution.

---

[2] The Act was not in force when the book was written.

negligent virus transmission

Damage to your own computer system can have serious repercussions for the running of your business. To avoid interruption to your business, all incoming e-mail messages should be checked

►►► **INFO POINT** 63 per cent of companies are concerned about cyberliability for negligent virus transmission.

for viruses. You should make sure that your insurance cover extends to cover such business interruption (see 'insurance policies', p.136).

With outgoing material, the accidental transmission to a third party of a virus could make your company liable to that third party for any damage caused as a result, if your company has been negligent in allowing the virus to be transmitted.

Under the Computer Misuse Act 1990, the deliberate introduction of a damaging virus is a criminal offence. Traditionally, viruses have been spread as a result of infected programs, computer games, shareware, etc. However, one of the greatest threats today is from 'macroviruses'. These viruses are distributed as macros in electronic documents, including e-mails.

All attachments to messages to a third party should be checked for viruses in the same way as incoming attachments. Where publicly available material, e.g. from the Internet, is transmitted to a third party, a suitable disclaimer should be included.

❝Under the Computer Misuse Act 1990, the deliberate introduction of a damaging virus is a criminal offence❞

disclosure of computer records in legal proceedings

E-mail messages are not always automatically destroyed when sent and read: they are often retained on the sender's e-mail system and the recipient's e-mail system until specifically destroyed.

Once legal proceedings begin, every party to those proceedings is obliged to preserve and disclose all documents (including e-mails) relevant to the dispute, whether or not they help its case.

Indeed, any party may apply to the court for an order compelling your company to preserve and hand over relevant e-mails. Appropriate

►►► **WARNING** If your company becomes party to legal proceedings, you could be compelled to disclose relevant e-mail messages held on your company's computer system.

disclaimers and corporate policy should help to ensure that there is no employee 'expectation of privacy', particularly in relation to company e-mail systems.

effective service

If a document is posted it may be considered to have been 'served' or delivered; that is, there is an implied guaranteed delivery and this is known as 'effective service'.

The Civil Procedures Rules state that service by 'electronic method' other than fax (which presumably includes e-mail) is deemed to be effected on the second day after the day on which the e-mail is transmitted. However, there are special rules defining when service by 'other electronic means' may take place, namely where:

1. the party serving the document and the party on whom it is to be served are both acting through a legal representative;

2. the document is served at the legal representative's business address;

3. the legal representative who is to be served has previously expressly indicated in writing to the party serving that he is willing to accept service by this means and has provided:

   - his e-mail address; or

   - other electronic identification (such as an ISDN or other phone link number).

An e-mail that does not meet all of the above criteria will not constitute effective service.

e-mail and company stationery

Under the Companies Act (1985 and 1989) and the Business Names Act (1985), there are certain requirements relating to the information that should be included in business correspondence and other documents.

Both Acts use the term 'business letters' to define one of the forms of communication to which their requirements apply. Since both Acts came into force before e-mail was widely used, it is not clear whether or not an e-mail would be considered as a business letter.

However, it would be prudent to assume that if an e-mail relates to company business, it will be subject to the same legal requirements as a traditional letter, namely that it should include:

- the company name, country of registration and registered number;

- its registered office address;

- the fact that it is a limited company (in the case of a limited company exempt from the obligation to use the word 'Limited' as part of its name).

Under the Business Names Act, there are further requirements for companies, individuals and partnerships using a business name. However they are beyond the scope of this book.

taking legal action

This chapter shows that the legal aspects of e-mail are wide ranging and their implications can be considerable. You should take steps to minimize the risk of facing legal proceedings. One of those steps is the subject of the next chapter: 'Developing a Business E-mail Policy'.

> ➤➤➤ HOT TIP 'Prevention is better than court.'
> *Theodore Goddard*

If, on the other hand, your company is the victim of an e-mail injustice, you may decide to take legal action. Indeed many companies have an excellent reputation and are prepared to fight hard to protect it. However, although the threat of legal action may prove a useful tactic, it can also be time consuming, costly and not without risk.

Another option before you resort to legal action is to use mediators, for example, the Centre for Dispute Resolution (CEDR) in the UK.

> ➤➤➤ WATCH POINT 'Don't go to court unless you have to. But if it means protecting your reputation, be prepared to do it.'
> *Julian Stainton*
> *Chief Executive, Western Provident Association*

These organizations act independently to help people in conflict to reach a settlement. It can also have the advantage of being quicker and cheaper than taking legal action through the courts.

answers to the questions worth asking

1. Can e-mail messages be used as evidence in a court of law?
   Yes. They can and they have been.

2. Should my company e-mail messages contain the same information as that on my company stationery (such as my registered office address and company registration number)?
   Yes. Although the relevant legislation does not explicitly refer to e-mail, it does refer to 'business letters' which could include e-mail.

3. Should I include a disclaimer on all e-mail messages that I send outside my company?
   Yes. However, not everything can be disclaimed. For example, you cannot disclaim liability for a libellous statement that you make.

4. Can I confirm a contract with a customer by sending them an e-mail message?
   Yes. You can also change a contract by e-mail.

5. If a customer sends me confidential information by e-mail is there anything that would prevent me from forwarding it to other people?
   Yes. You may be in breach of confidence.

6. As an employer, am I liable if, for example, an employee is downloading from the Internet pornographic material that he/she is then forwarding around the office by e-mail?
   Yes. If it creates a 'hostile' workplace for your employees, they could take action against you.

7. As an employer, can I hold an employee responsible for any action that may result from something the employee puts in a message?
   Possibly. It depends on the terms of employment, company guidelines (such as codes of practice, company e-mail standards, etc.) and other relevant custom and practice. For example, if an employee's contract states that e-mail messages must not contain any defamatory material and an employee sends a message containing defamatory material, then the employee can be held liable.

8. **As an employer, am I entitled to look at my employees' e-mail messages?**

Yes. In the UK an employer can look at employees' messages, including personal messages, unless the employer has agreed not to. However, in the USA employees may well have rights of privacy. When the Human Rights Act 1998 comes into force, public sector employees in the UK may also have certain rights of privacy.

9. **As an employer, could I be liable if an employee sends a message containing a virus to a third party?**

Yes. Even accidental transmission to a third party of a virus would make you liable if you have been negligent in allowing the virus to be transmitted.

10. **Can I serve legal documents by e-mail?**

Yes. However, you would have to issue them through a legal representative and there are a number of conditions that must be satisfied.

11. **Is it unlawful to send an e-mail using someone else's e-mail address?**

Possibly. It may well be unlawful if by doing so the 'hoaxer' has committed an unlawful act such as sending a libellous message.

12. **If I forward an e-mail message that contains libellous allegations, can action be taken against me?**

Yes. Action can be taken against anyone who forwards the message as well as the person who wrote it.

13. **If I receive an e-mail message can I copy part of it and use it in other material?**

By doing so you may be infringing the copyright and so you would need to check first. In the UK, employers usually own the copyright in material created by an employee in the course of their work (which includes company e-mail messages).

14. **If I receive a libellous (or other offensive) message from someone who is in another country, and I want to take action against them, which law applies – the law of their country or the law of mine?**

The law of the country where the message is 'published'; that is, the law of the country where you download the material.

summary

The growth in the use of e-mail, and the Internet in general, is resulting in developments in current law. However, until more cases have been put before the courts, it is too early to predict how the law will be interpreted.

Many business e-mail users have already found themselves on the wrong side of the law, often without even knowing they were doing something unlawful. However, action has generally been taken against the employers rather than the employees – probably because there was more to be gained by doing so.

The legal issues are wide ranging and your business will be more vulnerable to legal action if it does not recognize all of them and take appropriate steps to protect itself.

developing a business e-mail policy

➤ **at a glance**

the need for a business e-mail policy

when to create a policy

what steps to take

what makes a good policy?

who to involve

communicating the policy

reviewing existing policies and procedures

beyond a policy

summary

**‟ By having
a business
e-mail policy
you can
give your
employees a
framework
within which
they can
operate ”**

the need for a business e-mail policy

E-mail is a fast developing business tool and you cannot expect your employees to know and understand all the risks and benefits of e-mail systems. By having a business e-mail policy you can give your employees a framework within which they can operate. It can give answers to the questions that are often left unanswered:

● Can I send personal messages using the company's e-mail system?

● Can I just sign the message in my own name or should I include some company information?

● Should I use the e-mail system in preference to other forms of communication?

● How long should I keep the messages that I send and receive?

● How can I make sure that the messages I send and receive do not contain a virus?

▶▶▶ INFO POINT 34 per cent of businesses have no company policy in relation to the use of external e-mail and the Internet.

By not answering questions like these you may be causing uncertainty and confusion among employees and therefore be exposing your business to intentional or unintentional misuse. You might not be using your e-mail system and, more importantly, your employees productively.

Furthermore, because e-mail is often thought of as an informal way of communicating, employees are not always aware of the risks that can result from misuse of the e-mail system.

>>> EXAMPLE Legal experts have urged employers to issue staff with formal e-mail guidelines following a £101,000 libel settlement in the High Court. The case has highlighted employers' vulnerability to legal action when staff make misleading or critical remarks in e-mails. Gas distribution firm BG paid damages to settle a case brought by a rival after a BG senior manager sent an e-mail to staff raising questions about their rivals' integrity.

Source: Computer Weekly

" The informality of e-mail can lead to messages being sent that are unsuitable, unnecessary or even illegal "

For example, external messages (to customers, suppliers and so on) may not be created with the same degree of importance as letters written on company stationery. With company stationery you are reminded that it is a 'formal' correspondence – the company name, address and other details are clearly visible. However, e-mail systems do not have the same kind of reminder.

The informality of e-mail can lead to messages being sent that are unsuitable, unnecessary or even illegal.

If you have an IT system that is an important part of your business (such as your bookkeeping system) you are unlikely to allow an untrained person to use it. However, this is exactly what many businesses that use e-mail are doing – their employees are using e-mail but they are not being guided on how to use it. The guidance they are given is often technical help about the e-mail system itself, such as how to send and receive messages and how to attach files.

alternative approaches to managing e-mail risks

So what options do you have for managing the risks that e-mail presents? Generally, for any risk, you have four options.

1. *Accept it.*   Accept that the risk may occur and that you can cope with its consequences.

2. *Avoid it.*   Do not put yourself in a position where it can occur, or if it does occur you will not be affected by it. In the case of e-mail you might choose not to use it at all.

3. *Reduce it.*   Take steps to minimize the chance of it occurring, or if it does occur minimize the effect that it may have.

4. *Move it.*   Move the effect of the risk somewhere else, for example, by taking out an insurance policy that covers business interruption. However, this will cover only part of the risk and so you may still be affected, although to a lesser degree.

If you intend to take full advantage of e-mail, then your main option will be to reduce the risk. One way you can do this is to develop a business e-mail policy

You can also develop contingency plans that you can follow if the risk actually happens and you are affected by it.

Any of these options could apply to your business and in practice you may choose to adopt more than one. However, if you intend to take full advantage of e-mail, then your main option will be to reduce the risk. One way you can do this is to develop a business e-mail policy.

what is an e-mail policy?

A business e-mail policy is a set of statements about how you want employees to use e-mail in your business. A good e-mail policy will:

- highlight the main risks to your business
- help to minimize the chance of them occurring.

Before you create a policy you should understand the risks and how you can use a policy to address them – and that is how this chapter is structured.

A 'policy' could also be referred to as standards, guidelines, regulations, directives or other terminology that you use in your business. What you call it is not as important as its purpose.

If you already have an e-mail policy you may need to update it. On p.132 there is a checklist that you can use to see if you need to review your existing policy.

understanding the risks

Previous chapters discussed the various risks that businesses face if they use e-mail. For example:

- getting infected from viruses contained in attachments, and infecting others;
- clogging corporate networks by sending high volume, low value messages, and messages with unusually large attachments;
- sending libellous, sexist, racist or other potentially illegal material within a message;
- revealing sensitive company information;
- disclosing personal information;
- entering into a legal contract unintentionally;
- time wasting by sending and receiving unnecessary messages.

Employees are not always aware that their messages can bring these risks to their organization.

> **" Employees are not always aware that their messages can bring risks to their organization "**

If any of these risks did occur in your business, the effect may do no more than briefly disrupt your day-to-day operation on one particular day. For example, you may have to send a 'gentle' reminder to staff about their use of the company's e-mail system. However, at the other end of the scale you may be subjected to a lengthy and costly legal dispute that could affect the profit and reputation of your company.

Of course the risks listed above are not all unique to e-mail. If, for example, you were planning the launch of a new product, there might not be much you could do to prevent a disgruntled employee from sending a letter, using your company headed stationery, to your main competitor or even to the media. Although you may take action against the employee, the damage will already have been done. Similarly, an employee could load some software onto the office PC using a diskette brought from home. If the software contained a virus, you could be faced with the task of disinfecting your PC and any other PCs to which it may have spread. Neither of these two examples depends on e-mail. The difference with e-mail is that, because of its informal nature, employees may not even be aware that they are taking risks. A good policy will raise awareness.

▶▶▶ **INFO POINT** 67 per cent of small to medium-sized companies do not have a published e-mail policy.

Source: InTuition

❝ If you use an internal e-mail system but not a public one, you still need a business e-mail policy❞

a policy for internal and external e-mail

If you use an internal e-mail system but not a public one, you still need a business e-mail policy. Just because you have a secure network and your messages can only be sent and received within your company, it does not mean that all the risks are removed. Although some of them are removed others remain, for example, time wasted sending and receiving unnecessary messages.

If you use an ISP they are likely to have Terms and Conditions that you agree to follow. You are unlikely to get access to their e-mail servers unless you have agreed to follow them.

maximizing the benefits of e-mail

Although a policy will help to manage the risks, you should also be thinking of the benefits that e-mail brings to your business. A policy can help you to maximize those benefits. It can help to:

● improve your internal communications

● develop a closer, more interactive relationship with your customers

● improve your productivity

● reduce your costs.

Do not only think of a policy as a way of stopping the things that you do not want to happen, but also think of using it to encourage the things that you do want to happen. For example, you should encourage users to:

● promote the image of your company – by creating professional messages;

● check their messages regularly – there is no point in sending an important message to all your staff if one or more of them does not bother to read their messages. Similarly, if a customer sends you a message they will expect a reply within a reasonable timeframe;

● reduce the amount of paper your company uses – by distributing information electronically.

effect of company size

Do you need a policy if you are a company of one employee and a company of, say, 1,000 employees? Yes – what might differ is the level of formality that you give to your policy.

For example, if you are a one-person company your policy may be little more than a gentle reminder to yourself of 'the rules of good e-mail messages' given on p.68. You might even keep the checklist of questions by your PC (see p.161). However, if you run a company of 1,000 employees, you should have a documented policy that is referenced in your staff procedures manual or other relevant material.

when to create a policy

An independent survey of 200 UK companies with a turnover of £25m or more is summarized in Figure 6.1.

Figure 6.1 shows that although more than 90 per cent of the businesses surveyed used e-mail to send messages externally, only two-thirds of them had an e-mail policy in place. This is consistent with InTuition's findings (see p.120).

Unfortunately these surveys did not go as far as establishing how these businesses were managing their e-mail risks. The companies may all have decided to accept the effect of the risks if they occurred and/or take out insurance to cover themselves. However, this is unlikely. An e-mail policy can and should be used to manage business risks. These businesses were not managing their risks effectively.

Some companies may consider a policy to be unnecessary as they may have only a few people using e-mail. However, over time the use of e-mail spreads throughout the whole company and still there is no policy in place. By the time a policy is introduced, bad habits have already developed and it may take time to correct them.

❝Do you need a policy if you are a company of one employee and a company of, say, 1,000 employees? Yes – what might differ is the level of formality that you give to your policy❞

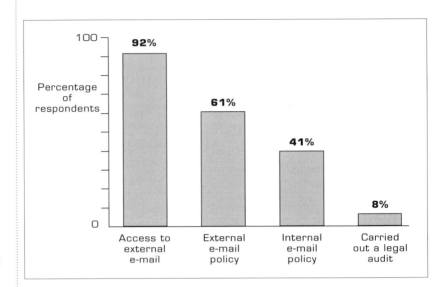

Fig 6.1
Summary of legal survey

Source: QA Research (for Theodore Goddard, Integralis and Alexander Forbes Risk Services)

> **"A policy will be easier to implement if it is implemented early"**

A policy will be easier to implement if it is implemented early. Ideally, you should implement your policy before you start using e-mail. However, as the above survey suggests, many businesses either do not bother with a policy or only implement it after they have started using e-mail. It is better to have a policy later, than not at all.

what steps to take

Fig 6.2 shows the steps to follow to create a policy.

The amount of time that you spend creating your policy will depend on a number of factors including:

- the risks and benefits of e-mail to your business
- the size of your business (in terms of the number of employees)
- the number of employees using e-mail
- whether you can send and receive external e-mail.

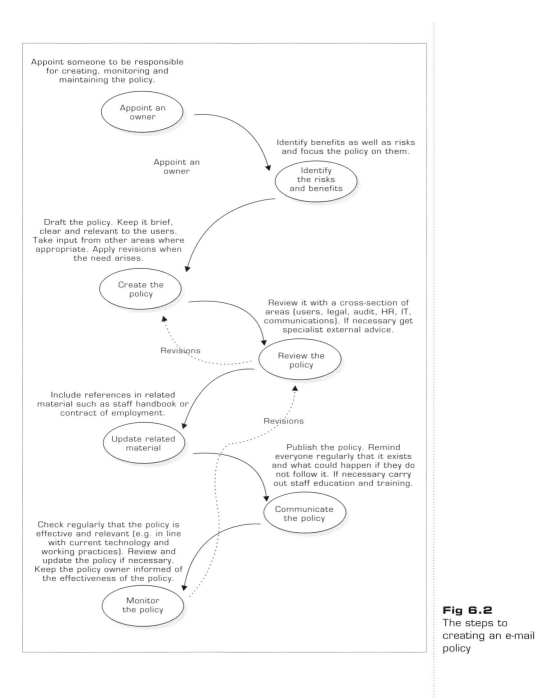

Appoint someone to be responsible for creating, monitoring and maintaining the policy.

Appoint an owner

Appoint an owner

Identify benefits as well as risks and focus the policy on them.

Identify the risks and benefits

Draft the policy. Keep it brief, clear and relevant to the users. Take input from other areas where appropriate. Apply revisions when the need arises.

Create the policy

Review it with a cross-section of areas (users, legal, audit, HR, IT, communications). If necessary get specialist external advice.

Revisions

Review the policy

Include references in related material such as staff handbook or contract of employment.

Revisions

Update related material

Publish the policy. Remind everyone regularly that it exists and what could happen if they do not follow it. If necessary carry out staff education and training.

Communicate the policy

Check regularly that the policy is effective and relevant (e.g. in line with current technology and working practices). Review and update the policy if necessary. Keep the policy owner informed of the effectiveness of the policy.

Monitor the policy

Fig 6.2
The steps to creating an e-mail policy

"Make someone responsible for developing the policy and for making sure that it is effective"

Make someone responsible for developing the policy and for making sure that it is effective.

For UK companies bear in mind that directors have a duty to their company. If you are a director and you do not have a business e-mail policy you could be liable for the actions of your employees.

what makes a good policy?

the contents of a good policy

A good policy will give your business the flexibility to get the very best out of your investment. There is no single policy that is suitable for every business. Each business has some unique characteristics in its culture and the way that it operates and your policy should reflect that uniqueness.

There is no point in just copying a policy verbatim from somewhere else. You will benefit from understanding your own needs and desires and basing your policy on them. Although there is no definitive list, as a minimum you should consider covering the following topics:

- risks and benefits of e-mail to your company

- security and confidentiality

- legal status of e-mail messages

- any distinctions between handling internal and external messages

- information that should be included in external messages (such as disclaimers and company contact details)

- use of e-mail for personal matters

- management (including storage, archiving, retrieval and deletion of messages sent and received)

- manner and tone of messages

- references to company standards and best practice guidelines

- personal responsibilities of every e-mail user

- monitoring and control of the e-mail system

- procedures for handling inappropriate messages that are received (for example, messages containing sexist or racist material)

- possible consequences of ignoring the policy.

❝You should make your policy brief but specific❞

You should make your policy brief but specific (see Appendix C, p.171 for some sample policies). Be clear about the consequences of disregarding the policy. You might want to consider varying levels of action, for example:

- sending jokes – oral warning

- sending material which is offensive – written warning

- intentionally distributing a virus – instant dismissal and possible legal action.

Consequently you may also have to fit in with, or revise, an existing staff policy. Some companies combine their e-mail policy with other policies such as those covering security or Internet access. Although there may be valid reasons for doing this, if you want your policy to be clear to all your employees, it may not help to combine these topics.

characteristics of a good policy

A good policy is one that is:

- clearly written

- practical and contains realistic examples

- flexible – it can be updated relatively easily

- easy to access – does not require much effort to find it

- suggestive, not aggressive – gives the impression of seeking co-operation rather than being dictatorial

- brief but unambiguous.

> ➤➤➤ **WATCH POINT** There is a tendency for technical staff to create the policy because e-mail is an IT system. However, there is a danger that it will be written for a technical audience – the technician assumes that everyone will know what they are talking about.

Try and keep your policy to no more than about 1,500 words – which equates to, say, two or three sides of A4 (US letter).

You should also get input from others when you create the policy (see 'who to involve', p.127).

> ➤➤➤ **CASE STUDY** A company's policy was created by the company's security section because they considered security to be their greatest risk. The policy stated that 'secret information must be encrypted'. However, when employees were asked about how they would encrypt secret information, none of them knew. There was also a great debate about what constituted 'secret' information.
>
> The policy failed on two counts: it did not explain the problem and it did not give a solution – it gave a theoretical expectation. Why was it theoretical? Because the company's e-mail system did not support encryption.

As with your e-mail messages, your policy should be written in plain language. Finally, a good policy is one that is monitored. Just because you develop a business e-mail policy it does not mean that you have done your job. There is little point putting a policy in place if you do not then check that the policy is effective. You should check regularly that your policy is:

❝As with your e-mail messages, your policy should be written in plain language❞

● being followed

● up to date.

You can adopt the three Ps: Policy – Practice – Patrol. Say what you want to happen, make it happen, check that it is continuing to happen.

Let your staff know how the system is being used. If, for example, you fire an employee because of gross misuse of your company's e-mail system, you may want to remind your staff that misuse can result in the termination of employment.

who to involve

The majority of the risks of e-mail do not relate directly to IT – they are HR (human resources), legal or general business risks. Therefore when you create a business e-mail policy you should involve people from these, and possibly other, disciplines. There are two good reasons for doing this:

1. You get input from experts.

2. It helps to foster a sense of ownership of the policy – it is a company policy, not an IT or other unit's policy.

Who you involve will depend on the size of your organization. Point two is more relevant to a large organization, where there may be separate people responsible for HR, legal, IT and other functions. If, on the other hand, you are a sole trader you may want to obtain external professional guidance.

Here is a list of the functions that you should consider involving:

- HR
- IT
- legal
- audit
- users
- communications
- trade unions, staff bodies.

Everyone that you involve may be an e-mail user so you can get them to 'road test' your policy.

Large companies in particular can be very protective with their corporate communications, with a well-documented approval process and only a 'chosen few' being allowed to talk to the media. However, a few keystrokes from a disgruntled employee could mean your company's name is mud all over the world.

communicating the policy

There are a number of ways that you can communicate and reinforce your policy. Depending on the size of your company you may select one, many or even all of these.

If you are a company with your own e-mail system, you should make sure that all users see and 'sign up' to the policy, including contract staff and temporary staff or anyone else who you allow to use your e-mail system. The main ways that you can communicate your policy include:

- paper-based document
- Intranet-based document
- signed declaration
- on-screen click notices
- staff education and training
- videotape messages.

paper-based document

Produce the policy on paper and make sure that there is a copy in each office, or give each member of staff their own copy. Some companies have had fanfold leaflets or aide-mémoire cards professionally produced and given them to all staff.

intranet-based document

For those companies that have an Intranet, create an HTML format document and publish it.

This has the added advantage of being able to include hypertext links to related material.

If you have a secure web site that only your company can access, you could publish it there.

signed declaration

Before giving access to the e-mail system (that is, before issuing a UserId and password) you can ask staff to read and sign the policy.

Fig 6.3 shows a sample document that a company asked all its e-mail users to sign (but only after some 'incidents' had occurred).

OurCompany
E-mail user agreement

The technology provided by OurCompany for you to do your job is OurCompany property. It is made available for you to use for business purposes only.

Inappropriate use of technology including misuse of the e-mail or the Internet for non-business purposes will not be tolerated. Such actions could be viewed by OurCompany as Gross Misconduct and in certain circumstances could lead to dismissal. OurCompany has dismissed members of staff for computer misuse.

OurCompany is now able to monitor usage of its technology and with immediate effect frequent, random monitoring will be undertaken.

If you receive an inappropriate message, it should be deleted on receipt and reported. The onward transmission of non-work related material is not permitted.

Every member of staff within OurCompany will be given a copy of this note and be requested to sign and return it to OurCompany to acknowledge that there is no doubt as to the company's requirements in this respect.

Signed: _____ Date: _____

Fig 6.3
Sample signed
declaration

on-screen 'click on' notices

When you subscribe to an ISP you usually have to agree to their Terms and Conditions as a part of sign-up process. If you do not agree to them, you cannot sign up.

You can apply a similar principle in your own company. For example, as part of the log-on process to a company network you can display a notice reminding staff of the policy and highlighting key aspects of it. Fig 6.4 is an example that is used by a UK-based company.

Use of e-mail

OurCompany can inspect any message which is sent or received by its e-mail systems.

Misuse of the e-mail systems may result in disciplinary action.

There are clear and explicit guidelines regarding the sending of secret information.

Fig 6.4
On-screen 'click on' notice

staff education and training

You should include your policy in e-mail and other communications training courses.

If you have a joining pack for new employees, you could also include a copy of the policy in it.

videotape messages

Some companies, especially large companies, produce video messages that staff are asked to watch.

In addition to the above ways of communicating your policy, you can use existing communication channels, such as:

- team, unit, office, department, division meetings

- newsletters and company magazines

- Intranets

- e-mail broadcasts.

You will also need to involve staff (and unions, if necessary) if you intend to update:

- staff contracts of employment

- staff handbook/process manuals

- disciplinary procedures.

You might also consider giving 'weight' to the publication by including a message from a senior person.

    You should also remind staff regularly of your policy. Despite our best intentions we can all develop bad habits and once we have them they are difficult to shake off. Some companies circulate their policy periodically and ask their employees to sign a form to show that they have read the policy.

    Try and vary the way that you remind staff. Familiarity breeds contempt – if you see the same notice regularly, it is easy to 'switch off' assuming that you know the content and therefore do not need reminding of it.

❝ You should also remind staff regularly of your policy❞

reviewing existing policies and procedures

reviewing an existing e-mail policy

If you already have a policy and you answer 'no' to any of the questions in Table 6.1 you may need to take the action suggested.

Question	Answer		Action
1. Is the policy easily accessible to all staff on a day-to-day basis?	No	⇨	Review the way that the policy is made available to staff. Make it easy for them to find it and use it. Make sure it is easy to understand.
2. Are staff reminded regularly of the policy (at least every three months)?	No	⇨	Revise your communication strategy to make sure that the policy, and the importance of it, is reinforced to staff. Diarize a regular reminder.
3. Is the content of the policy reviewed regularly (at least every six months) and updated to reflect changes in: ● technology ● the law, *and* ● your business processes?	No	⇨	Diarize to review and, if necessary, update the policy at least twice a year.
4. To check the policy is being followed, is there an audit conducted (at least every six months)?	No	⇨	Conduct an audit and act on the findings of it.
5. Is the policy reviewed each time it is broken?	No	⇨	Review the policy to make sure that the policy was clear – if necessary, give realistic examples to explain.
6. Is the policy reviewed each time there is an incident that is not covered by the policy?	No	⇨	Revise the policy and communicate it to staff.
7. Does the policy cover all the points listed in the section 'the contents of a good policy'? (see p.124)	No	⇨	Review the policy and include the missing points where appropriate.

Table 6.1
E-mail policy
review

reviewing related material

You may have to update other related material to refer to your policy. Possible material includes:

1. *Staff contracts of employment*: for example, you may want to make it a contractual right to be able to monitor e-mail messages sent and received by employees.

2. *Staff 'procedures' manuals*: for example, you may want to:

   - include standards and guidelines to be followed when using the company's e-mail system;

   - refer to the e-mail standards and guidelines within other procedures. For example, you may have a process for raising purchase orders and want to extend that process to include orders raised by e-mail.

3. *Disciplinary procedures*: for example, you may want to update your disciplinary procedures.

If you make changes to an existing policy you should also consider the above points.

beyond a policy

Although a business e-mail policy is important to have, it may not be enough in its own right. There are further steps that you can take, for example:

- provide education and training

- include disclaimers and other information on messages

- install software (such as message content checkers) to control its use

- take out insurance cover.

Each of these steps is discussed in the following sections.

staff education and training

>>> **INFO POINT** 59 per cent of companies do not provide e-mail or Internet usage guidelines to new staff.

In addition to covering the technical side of e-mail, training should also refer to your e-mail policy. It you want your staff to use e-mail effectively it is important that they understand its strengths and weaknesses and also the way that your company wants them to use e-mail.

disclaimers and confidentiality notices

ff In addition to covering the technical side of e-mail, training should also refer to your e-mail policy 99

>>> **CASE STUDY** E-mail delivers better results in British Airways (BA)
More than 2 million e-mails a week threatened to overload British Airways' networks and its people. BA asked The Marketing & Communication Agency Ltd (MCA)[1] to help staff solve the problem.

BA was moving from three different e-mail systems to a single system and saw a chance to encourage more effective e-mail habits. BA wanted to keep up the enthusiasm for using e-mail, but channel it into best practices.

MCA launched a four-pronged campaign:

- a paper-based newspaper ('The Daily E-mail') including valuable e-mail tips

- a short video showing some common e-mail habits that overly burdened the system (such as leaving an Inbox overflowing with e-mails or sending extremely large files as attachments)

- a touring exhibition with rolling presentations and a PC clinic with five-minute 'ability boosters'

- a questionnaire given to people at the exhibition explored their e-mail usage and a few months later a follow-up questionnaire was sent.

In addition, system changes were made which made it easier for people to follow best practice. For example, department logos at the top of e-mails took up a lot of memory, so they were replaced with separate and much simpler headers.

However, old habits die hard, so BA continues to present smaller versions of the exhibition around the world and reminds people of good e-mail habits through its Internet site.

1 MCA is an international consulting firm that helps organizations to align their staff with business goals and achieve successful change.

Should your messages include legal disclaimers and confidentiality notices? Unfortunately there is no clear-cut answer. Legal professionals might well say that you must and if you want to cover every possible eventuality then you probably should.

> **>>> INFO POINT** Employers and employees are unaware of the legal implications of e-mail.
>
> 73 per cent of companies do not include disclaimers or warnings of any kind on their e-mail transmissions.

However, there is a price to pay if you decide to include these notices – your one-line message to confirm a meeting with a customer could turn into a screen of legal notices. But you might say that it is easy to ignore all the notices after the message. In response to that, some people might consider that you should include them at the start of your message because they are important and you want people to read them – and if they are not important, then why are they in your message?

> **>>> WATCH POINT** You should note that although disclaimers are recommended, you cannot disclaim against everything. For example, you cannot disclaim against a libellous statement that you make.

Most e-mail systems now allow you to add a 'signature' to your messages automatically and you can use this to include the information that you put in all your messages.

You may include different information depending on whether your message is internal or external. Beware that what might start off as an internal message could be copied externally, without you knowing it.

If you are in any doubt as to whether or not you should include a notice, then you should include one. If you are in any doubt about what the notice should say, you should get legal advice (see Appendix D, p.183 for some example notices). Do not forget that in the UK you should include your company details in your e-mail messages (see p.110).

> **If you are in any doubt as to whether or not you should include a notice, then you should include one. If you are in any doubt about what the notice should say, you should get legal advice**

firewalls and filters

If you are using firewalls and filters to block and monitor incoming and outgoing messages, then you should make sure they are configured in accordance with your policy (see 'filters', p.62 and 'firewalls', p.81).

insurance policies

As the use of e-mail increases the risks to your business, you should consider the need to update your insurance policy, or if you do not have one consider the need for one.

Policies exist which include the following cover:

▶▶▶ INFO POINT 79 per cent of UK businesses either have no insurance cover for cyberliability or do not know whether they have such cover.

- infringement of intellectual property

▶▶▶ HOT TIP E-mail (and e-commerce in general) is revolutionizing the way business is conducted.

Businesses should re-assess their existing insurance policies and consider the true extent to which they are insured against cybercrime.

Alexander Forbes Risk Services

---

rights including copyright, patent or trademark or moral rights, or an act of passing off;

- breach of confidence or infringement of any right to privacy;

- misuse of any information which is either confidential or subject to statutory restrictions in use (such as confidential payroll data);

- defamatory statements;

- inadvertent and negligent virus transmission;

- fraudulent use of a company's own electronic signature or electronic mail.

summary

Your policy should be designed to minimize the likelihood of risks occurring and, if they do occur, minimizing the effect of them. Furthermore, you should aim to maximize the benefits of using e-mail. Therefore you need to identify the risks and benefits to your business.

Every business is unique in some way and so the risks and benefits of the way that you use e-mail will also be unique. You should decide on what is important to you and focus on that.

Your company policy should not be a stand-alone item. You should supplement it with training, confidentiality notices and disclaimers, and insurance cover where it is appropriate.

A policy is of limited value if its effectiveness is not monitored and if it does not change with the times. So creating an effective policy is just the start of managing the effectiveness of e-mail in your business.

creating good messages

> **at a glance**

what makes a good message?

the purpose of your message

addressing messages

message structure

attaching files to messages

writing clearly

protecting messages

other features of e-mail messages

rules of good e-mail messages

summary

what makes a good message?

>>> INFO POINT 'Netiquette' is e-mail etiquette – that is, the dos and don'ts of e-mail messages – which is the subject of this chapter.

What makes a good e-mail message? A good message normally displays the six characteristics listed here.

1. A good message has a definite purpose.

2. A good message is properly addressed.

3. A good message is well structured.

4. A good message is written clearly.

5. A good message uses attachments wisely.

6. A good message is protected appropriately.

❝A good message is written with common sense❞

Above all a good message is written with common sense. A good message gets the best out of what e-mail offers. It takes advantage of its availability, its speed, its cost and its ability to distribute information efficiently.

However, many business messages fall short of their goal because one or more of the six characteristics listed above has been overlooked. For example:

- You may not know why it was copied to you.

- You may have to read through forty lines of text to find out the purpose of the message.

- You may not understand some of the terminology used.

- It may contain personal information about another person which you should not have seen.

- it may include an attachment that you cannot open.

Business letters tend to be formal and the sender can even appear to be pompous. With e-mail messages the pendulum seems to have swung in the opposite direction – messages are often more like unstructured written conversation.

One of the main reasons for the informality of e-mail messages is the speed of e-mail, which makes it more conversational than writing a letter. If you send a letter you may have to wait three or four days for a response – and for international mail it could take weeks. With e-mail you might expect a response within three or four hours or even minutes.

Each of these six characteristics is discussed in the following sections.

the purpose of your message

Having a purpose to your message may seem obvious – who is going to send a message without a reason? But have you ever received a message but not known why it was sent to you? Do you ever get the feeling that people copy you in on messages just because it is easy to do?

Have you ever received a message that attempts to fulfil many different purposes at once? The result is often confusion and a train of subsequent messages.

Ask yourself: what do you expect to happen as a result of you sending your message. Make sure your message is focused on achieving it. By having a single definite purpose to your message, it will clarify:

- the right recipients

- the right Cc: list

- the message structure

- the message content

- the style and tone of the message

- the timing of the message.

As well as the main purpose of your message, there may also be an underlying purpose. For example, in your message to a potential customer an underlying

❝Ask yourself: what do you expect to happen as a result of you sending your message. Make sure your message is focused on achieving it❞

purpose will be to create a good impression. If you are replying to a customer complaint, your response may also be protecting the image of your company.

When you reply to messages you should consider whether you need:

- to reply (is a reply necessary or expected?);
- to copy the message to all the people who received the original message;
- to include the original message as part of your reply.

If you want to forward a message that you have received you may need to check with the originator beforehand. The originator may not have wanted anyone else to see the message other than the person he or she addressed it to. If you do not want anyone other than the addressees to receive a message that you send, say so in your message or in the subject line. (This would be similar to putting 'Private and Confidential' on a envelope.)

addressing messages

address lines

Usually you can either key the e-mail addresses straight into the To: and Cc: lines or you can pick the addresses from an 'Address book' or 'Distribution list'.

Some systems have a Bcc: (Blind carbon copy) line. The people you list in this line will receive a copy of your message but anyone listed in the To: and Cc: lines will not see the names that you listed in the Bcc: line.

>>> **INFO POINT Addressing messages to large numbers of people** There are software products available which enable you to send many copies of a message without divulging the complete list of addressees to the recipients. These products give your messages a 'one-to-one' appearance.

" The purpose of your message should determine the recipients "

The purpose of your message should determine the recipients. Try to avoid sending messages with a long list of recipients. Although it might be easy to do, it can be annoying for the recipients if there are screens full of addresses to wade through before getting to the message itself. Also, if you are using more than one address list, check that names are not duplicated in those lists.

If you expect anyone on the Cc: list to take specific action as a result of receiving your message, then you should make it clear in the message. Otherwise recipients in the Cc: list might assume that the message is 'for information only'.

There can be a temptation to copy messages just because it is easy to do. However, you should only send messages to people who need to receive them – do not copy them unnecessarily.

Some companies insist that internal messages are not copied outside the company – they state that separate messages should be created. One of the advantages of doing this is that many company e-mail systems are configured automatically to append disclaimers to all external messages.

subject line

A good subject line helps to categorize a message whereas a bad one can be worthless to the recipient and to you. The recipient can gauge the importance of the message if you give it an appropriate subject line.

Your message may be just one of many that the recipients receive each day. It may be one of hundreds sitting in a message folder (such as an Inbox or Sent mail folder). A good subject line is one that is:

- meaningful
- relevant
- concise.

meaningful subject line

The subject line should give an indication of the context of the message. A poor subject line is almost worthless. For example:

    Subject: Information

However, the subject line below might give your communication a better chance:

    Subject: Launch of Gold Service Plan (GSP)

See also 'assigning a priority to a message', p.154.

❝The subject line should give an indication of the context of the message❞

relevant subject line

The subject line should be appropriate to the content of the message. You should avoid subject lines that aim to be attention grabbing but do not relate to the message content. For example:

```
Subject:  Boss caught with pants down
Message:  Now that I have your complete attention …
```

This type of subject line can be very frustrating, particularly for a busy e-mail reader.

concise subject line

The subject line should use the available space wisely. Subject lines do not necessarily have to be whole sentences, complete with punctuation. As there is limited space, the challenge is to use it wisely. Newspaper headlines are rarely complete sentences, but in a few easy to understand words they usually give a good indication of what you can expect to read in the related article.

The e-mail system you use may limit the size of the subject line. Also, the amount of the subject line that is visible on your screen may also vary. You may be able to alter the width of the subject line when you are viewing the contents of folders. Therefore, limit the size of your subject lines to, say, 40 characters.

A truncated subject line can give a whole new meaning to a message. Consider the following:

```
Subject:  20 per cent pay rise for all Marketing and
          Sales staff
```

The actual subject line was:

```
Subject:  20 per cent pay rise for all Marketing and
          Sales staff was rejected outright by
          management
```

The subject line should be a précis of the message and not an extract

The subject line should be a précis of the message and not an extract. Applying this to the above example might result in:

```
Subject:  20 per cent pay rise rejected
```

message structure

greeting (or salutation)

To many people the inclusion of a greeting or salutation (for example, Mike or Dear John) is unnecessary, whereas others prefer it. Some people consider the existence of a greeting to be formal, while others consider it to be informal. Two specific benefits of including a greeting are:

1. It acts as a double check to the recipients that the message was indeed intended for them.

   For example, if the message has been sent to the wrong e-mail address it should be apparent to the actual recipient as soon as he or she starts reading the message.

2. It clarifies the context in which the message has been sent to the recipient. If the message was copied to the recipient, they would not necessarily know that it was copied to them without looking first at the Cc: list.

If you decide to include a greeting the style will depend on several factors, including:

- how well you know the recipient

- how many recipients there are

- how often you send messages to the recipients

- the 'environment' from which you are sending the message – your company may have a 'house style'

- your personal style or preferences and those of your recipient.

If you do not know the person then it is safer to include a greeting as the absence of a greeting can make the sender appear 'cold' or 'distant'.

   If you do not know the name of the recipient, their title or even their gender, then a useful greeting might not be possible.

   If you are replying to a message then the signature of the person that sent you the original message should guide you.

> **❝ If you do not know the person then it is safer to include a greeting as the absence of a greeting can make the sender appear 'cold' or 'distant' ❞**

close and signature

The 'close' refers to the word or phrase that you put before you sign off, for example, 'Regards'. 'Signature' refers to your name or whatever you wish to be known as at the end of your message, along with any related information such as your job title.

Like the greeting, feelings are mixed about the need for a close and signature. Books on letter-writing may tell you that if you start a letter with 'Dear Mr Douglas' then you should end the letter with 'Yours sincerely' followed by your name. If you start with 'Dear Sir' then you should end with 'Yours faithfully' followed by your name. While such rules may be appropriate for business letter-writing, they can be too formal for e-mail.

So, should you include a close and should you include your name, nickname or whatever you want to be known by? A safe starting point is:

1. If you do not know the person then you should at least include:

   ● a close – such as 'Regards'

   ● a signature – such as your first and last name.

2. If you include a greeting then you should also include either a close, your signature (at least your first name) or both. In other words, if you put something at the beginning, then put something at the end.

You may also want to include some additional information as part of your signature, for example:

   ● your job title

   ● the address of your company's web site.

Often the sender's additional information includes their company name, full postal address, phone number, fax number, business e-mail address and personal e-mail address. However, you should only include what you think is necessary (which may of course vary for different types of messages).

Another reason to include a signature is that without it the recipient may have no other information about you other than your e-mail address. The recipient should not have to spend as long thinking about the greeting in their reply if you have included a signature.

As with the greeting, your company may have a 'house style'. In which case you should apply it to your messages.

layout

Using spaces and blank lines can help the readability of your messages. Large blocks (or paragraphs) of text can appear rushed and uninviting, whereas smaller blocks with logical break points appear more achievable. Therefore, insert a blank line between:

- your greeting and the first line of your message

- each paragraph

- the last paragraph and your close

- your close and your signature.

If the layout of your text is important, the limitations of your or your recipient's text editor may mean that you have to consider creating the text in another way (such as by using a word processor). If this is the case, you may have to send your text as an attachment.

text format

The most straightforward text format is plain text. With plain text you are limited to the keys which appear on a standard keyboard and one font.

However, other formats include RTF (Rich Text Format) and HTML (which is becoming a popular standard format for e-mail messages). If your system supports these formats you can take advantage of their features such as different font styles (for example, bold, italic or underlined text), bulleted or numbered lists and text alignment (for example, centred, left or right justified).

Also, with HTML you can include e-mail addresses so that when the recipient clicks on the address their e-mail system automatically creates a new message and inserts the e-mail address. Similarly, if you include a web address, when the recipient clicks on the address the page is automatically displayed (through the recipient's Internet browser).

❝As with the greeting, your company may have a 'house style'. In which case you should apply it to your messages❞

Some e-mail systems have stationery templates that allow you to include a selection of text fonts and background images to the messages that you send.

➤➤➤ WATCH POINT The ability to send and receive HTML-formatted text is not common to all e-mail systems.

Even though you may be able to create HTML-formatted messages, your recipients may not be able to take full advantage of them.

If you send an HTML-formatted message and the recipient's e-mail system does not support it, they will see a plain text message. However, plain text might include many of the formatting characters that will detract from the 'readability' of the message.

Therefore, before you send an HTML-formatted message you should check that the recipient will be able to read it.

As with the layout of your text, if the text format is important to your message, you may have to produce the text as a separate file and 'attach' it to your e-mail message.

➤➤➤ WATCH POINT Do not write messages only in block capitals (upper case) or lower case. Use sentence case.

Text written in block capitals can seem aggressive, as though you are shouting at the recipient. Also, reading text in block capitals is more difficult than reading lower case text. People get used to the visual pattern of words (such as the difference in height between the upper case letters and lower case letters).

Using block capitals in subjects that contain a lot of acronyms (such as in the field of computing) can add further difficulty.

Also, text written solely in lower case can give the impression that it was rushed or even that the author was lazy.

Therefore use a sentence case with a proper mix of upper and lower case text.

attaching files to messages

The ability to attach files is one of the most powerful and popular features of e-mail. Attachments can come in all shapes and sizes, including word-processed documents, spreadsheets, program files, data files, static images, audio/video files or even complex dynamic images such as virtual reality files. If you can save it as a file you can attach it to a message.

However, as well as being one of the most popular facilities of e-mail, the ability to attach files is arguably the one that causes the most problems. For example, you may have:

- received an attachment but not been able to open it;

- received a message that referred to an attachment that did not exist;

- waited for a large attachment to download, opened it and then discovered that it was irrelevant to you and therefore a waste of your time;

▶▶▶ **WATCH POINT** **Make sure that you attach a file when you say that you are going to.** One of the most common mistakes is to say that you are attaching a file and then forget actually to attach it – it is easy enough to do.

Instead of attaching the file after you have written your message, you could attach it before you start typing, or when you type a reference to the attachment in your message.

- opened an attachment and subsequently discovered that it contained a virus.

When you attach files to messages you should consider:

- the type of attachment

- the name of the attachment

- the size of the attachment

- the number of attachments

- the importance of the information in the attachment

- viruses.

type of attachment – file types

One way to annoy the recipient of your message is to attach a file that they cannot open. It might also mean at least another two messages need to be sent, one from them to you to tell you that they cannot access the file, and another from you to them re-sending the file in a different format.

▶▶▶ **WATCH POINT** Before you send an attachment consider whether or not the person you are sending it to will be able to read it. If necessary, check that they have the right software and the right version of the software.

One common mistake is attaching files that have been created on the latest version of software that the recipient may not have. You may be an enthusiastic owner of the latest software release, but the recipient of your message may not share your enthusiasm when, after many attempts, they discover they are not able to open the attachment.

name of the attachment – file name

There are still many users whose operating systems will only recognize file names which are eight characters or less, with a three-character extension (for example, orders99.doc). If you send a file with a longer file name to these users, they may have to change the file name before they can open the file.

Also, the file extension is used to identify the application, so that when the person who is opening the file double-clicks on the file icon, the application starts and the file is opened. If you attach a file with an unusual file extension, the user may have to try and find the appropriate application themselves.

If you have more than one attachment, and their file names do not make it clear which file is which, refer to them in the message and give them their file names. For example:

> … and so I have attached the surveyor's full report (KT44.DOC) and the summary (KT43a.DOC).

File names which are meaningful to the recipient would of course be helpful – REPORT.DOC and SUMMARY.DOC in the above example.

size of the attachment

The cost of sending a letter by post is very much related to its size (more specifically its weight) and to a large extent the same can be said of e-mail messages. Both you and the recipient will pay (either in time or money or both – however inexpensive that might be) for the privilege of sending and receiving files as attachments. Although size may well become less of an issue in the future, for the time being you should be aware of file sizes.

Some companies discourage the use of attachments unless they are really necessary. They claim that attachments to messages can increase the size of the information that is sent over their private networks that can make their networks less efficient.

If you are attaching a large file (say 500Kb or more) you should consider compressing the files and if necessary checking that the recipient has the software to expand (or decompress) it. There is software that is popular for this purpose, for example Winzip® or Stuffit®. Using Winzip® it is possible to compress a 1Mb Microsoft® Word® file to 223Kb (a reduction of 80 per cent). You may also be able to compress the files so that they are self-extracting. With self-extracting files the recipient does not need the software necessary to decompress the files – it is automatically attached to the compressed file. When you create a self-extracting file with Winzip®, it creates an executable (.exe) file – that is, a file containing software that is ready to be run.

Alternatively, you may be able to place the file on a secure file store, for example, on a file server or an Intranet server, and in your message give a reference to where the document can be found. This has the advantage in that the recipient can decide if and when they actually want to view it.

➤➤➤ **INFO POINT** In Microsoft® Exchange® there is a facility to store only one copy of the attachment on the server. However, this only works if all the recipients are linked to the same server.

number of attachments

➤➤➤ **CASE STUDY** A company MD received an e-mail with twelve files attached to it. Each file made references to at least one of the other files and he soon got fed up with opening and reviewing attachments. The files covered four different applications and the combined size of the message and attachments was over three megabytes. The message was sent to about twenty recipients and the subsequent exchange of messages is too painful for him to recall.

Ideally you should attach no more than five files to your messages and even one or two can give problems to users with low speed links. Often the compression software (such as Winzip®) will enable you to include, as a single compressed file, the files that you want to attach.

Some service providers have limited the size of e-mail messages to, for example, 2Mb. Some have different limits for different types of accounts (for example, 2Mb for consumer accounts but no limit for commercial accounts).

❝If you are attaching a large file (say 500Kb or more) you should consider compressing the files and if necessary checking that the recipient has the software to expand (or decompress) it❞

Many organizations limit the size of messages that can pass through their internal systems.

format of the attachment

When you send an attachment, you may lose control over the format and content. So, for example, if you send someone a copy of your latest business case in Microsoft® Word® format, they may easily be able to copy parts of it into their own document. They could also change the layout of the document.

Although many systems allow you to produce read-only versions of files, it may still be possible for the recipient to open the file and then use a 'copy and paste' facility to copy data to another file that is not protected. One solution to this type of issue is to send the attachment as a Portable Data Format (PDF) file.

> ➤➤➤ **INFO POINT** PDF (Portable Document Format) is a file format created by Adobe Systems, who provide free reader software which allows you to view PDF files.
>
> Using PDF enables documents to be transmitted as an electronic image that is easily viewable on a PC.
>
> PDF files are especially useful for documents where the original graphical layout and appearance need to be preserved.

The format of the attachment can also affect its size. For example, here are the sizes of a 20-page document stored in a number of different formats:

Microsoft® Word® (.doc)	–	67Kb
Rich Text Format (.rtf)	–	104Kb
Text (.txt)	–	42Kb
Portable Data Format (.pdf)	–	62Kb

protecting attachments

If you attach a file that contains important information, you should protect it. (see 'attachments', p.85).

writing clearly

writing in plain language

It would be unpropitious if your electronic epistolary transmission was inefficacious, contrary to your prognostication.

In other words, it would be unfortunate if your e-mail message did not produce the effect you had expected.

In many ways our writing is just like our driving – over time we develop bad habits and our experiences and our environment influence us. Our aim should be to write clearly – in plain language.

Often businesses seem to have developed a language all of their own and business correspondence can be a breeding ground for 'official' language. Although e-mail does not appear as formal as letters, there are nevertheless many instances of notes that end with:

> Should you require any further information please do not hesitate to contact me.

This could easily be replaced with:

> Please contact me if you have any questions.

Writing clearly has a number of important benefits.

- It can save time for your reader – they will not have to decipher your message.

- It can avoid confusion – purpose, information and actions are unambiguous.

- It can create a good impression of you and your business – an effective message might be considered to be the sign of an effective business.

Writing clearly means getting your message across without the person on the receiving end having to work hard to understand it. Just because you understand what you have written does not mean that your recipients will understand it. Therefore, write in a style that your recipient will understand – write in their language.

As well as writing clearly, good grammar and correct spelling are also important. Many e-mail systems enable you automatically to check the spelling

❝Writing clearly means getting your message across without the person on the receiving end having to work hard to understand it❞

before sending messages. If you want to check the grammar and you have a word processor that has a grammar checker, you can copy your message and check it in the word processor. (Microsoft®Outlook® 2000 gives you the option of using Microsoft® Word® as your e-mail text editor and so you can use its spell checking and grammar checking facilities.)

international e-mail

E-mail seems to cross international boundaries as if they were not there. When you send a message it may not always be clear in which country the recipient is. Many Internet sites include an e-mail icon that you can just click on which will create a new blank message and generate the mail address for you. All you need to do is type in your message and hit the 'Send' key.

What might be perfectly sensible in your mother tongue may seem a little strange to someone whose first language is different from yours. Even within the same language variations can occur. For example, 'traffic lights' in the UK are 'signal lights' in the USA and 'traffic robots' in South Africa.

You should also take care if you use abbreviations, slang, humour and sarcasm. Even the level of formality can vary.

Two particular problems with international e-mail are:

1. *Date formats*: for example, consider 01/02/2000. Is this 1 February 2000 or 2 January 2000? The answer is: it depends.

   In the UK it is likely to be 1 February 2000 because the UK tends to use the day, month, year format DD/MM/YY, two digits for each of the day, month and year. However in the USA it is likely to be 2 January 2000 as the USA tends to use the month, day, year format MM/DD/YY.

2. *Monetary units* (that is, currencies): there are many countries that have the same name for their currency and so you may need to be explicit when you specify a monetary amount. Also, take care when using currency symbols (see 'symbols, special characters and abbreviations', p.156).

protecting messages

Every business wants to protect its important information. Therefore, because e-mail is not a totally secure method of communication, it is important that you protect your messages appropriately.

The security of e-mail is an important topic and you should refer to Chapter 4 for further details.

"Because e-mail is not a totally secure method of communication, it is important that you protect your messages appropriately**"**

other features of e-mail messages

assigning a priority to a message

Some e-mail systems allow you to assign a priority (such as 'low', 'medium' or 'high') to the messages that you send. The priority relates to the importance which the sender associates with the message and not to the speed of delivery.

Priorities are open to abuse. There is no benefit if every message in a busy office is sent 'high priority'.

However, the priority feature may not work unless the recipient of your message is using an e-mail system that supports this facility.

An alternative approach is to refer to the priority in the subject line, for example:

```
Subject:   IMPORTANT. 20 per cent pay rise rejected
```

> **▶▶▶ EXAMPLE** Western Provident Association allows its employees to use the e-mail system for personal mail.
> The subject line of all personal messages must start with 'SDP' (for Social, Domestic and Pleasure) which provides a clear distinction between business and private e-mail.

acknowledgement of receipt

How do you know if the message that you sent has been received? There are several ways of finding out.

- Phone them (or, in your message, ask them to phone you when they open the message).

- Ask them (in your message) to e-mail a brief message of confirmation.

- Use a 'receipt acknowledgement' facility.

  Some systems allow you to request an acknowledgement of receipt; when the recipient opens the messages for the first time an acknowledgement is sent automatically by the recipient's e-mail system to the sender.

  However, as with priorities, this feature may not work unless the recipient of your message is using an e-mail system that supports this facility.

If it is important that you know your message has been received, ask for an immediate response, for example, by e-mail or phone.

❝Because e-mail is written, it can be difficult to detect the tone of a message❞

smileys

Smileys are an example of 'emoticons' – icons that indicate emotion. Because e-mail is written, it can be difficult to detect the tone of a message. But e-mail users have not been put off by this limitation. On the contrary, 'smileys' have been used to compensate for it.

Smileys are standard text characters which, when they are used in a particular order, can show various forms of the smiley ☺ . Tilt your head left to see the effect of these examples:

❝Although smileys may have their place in an informal setting, you should not use them in business messages❞

```
:-)    a happy (or smiling) face
;-)    a wink
:-D    a shocked face
:-(    an unhappy face
8-)    a happy face wearing sunglasses
:-/    a puzzled face
```

Although smileys may have their place in an informal setting, you should not use them in business messages. There are several reasons for not using smileys:

- You might understand all the obscure smileys but that does not mean everyone else will.

- Humour can be very personal. What might seem funny to you might not be funny to someone else. Also, have you ever written something that you thought was funny at the time, but when you read it again some time later you realized that it was not funny and you then regretted having written it?

- In a business environment smileys may be considered unnecessary or even unprofessional.

symbols, special characters and abbreviations

To compensate for the limitations of text editors, some people use symbols to show emphasis. For example, you can use underscores to show underlining (it was a _great_ show) and asterisks to show missing letters (it was a cr*p show). Also, there are some special characters that do not travel well. In a message sent which contained the Trademark (™) symbol, by the time the message got to the recipient the ™ had become a full stop (.).

If you are in any doubt about how a character or symbol will appear to the recipient of your message, especially if you message is important, either:

- do not use it;

- if you do use it, spell it out

  for example £40(40 pounds) or just 40 pounds.

Some people use abbreviations in their messages, such as:

```
bfn      bye for now
cu       see you
imho     in my humble opinion
```

Although abbreviations may reduce the amount of keying that you have to do, you should be careful about using them in business messages. You may understand them but your recipient may not.

the date and time

The date and time is added to your message automatically by your PC or by your e-mail server. The recipient's e-mail server may also record the time that the message was received.

Unless you can always guarantee that the server's date and time are correct, each time you log onto your e-mail system you should check the date and time, especially if the date or time is important to you. Also, you should take account of time differences.

> **If the date or time is an important part of your message, consider including it as a part of the message itself**

If the date or time is an important part of your message, consider including it as a part of the message itself.

rules of good e-mail messages

addressing and subject lines

1. Avoid To: and Cc: lists that are very long (no more than 50 addresses in total.) If necessary use Distribution lists or other mail facilities to suppress the lists.

2. If you choose a recipient from a list such as an Address book or a Distribution list:

   - check that you have chosen the right one

   - check that the address in the list is up-to-date.

3. Only send messages to people who need to receive them.

4. Do not over-use the copy (Cc: and Bcc:) facilities.

5. Do not continue to copy a message if it has become a two-way conversation.

6. Make sure the subject line is meaningful, relevant and concise (40 characters is a useful limit).

7. If your message is important you should give it an appropriate label in the subject line.

greeting, close and signature

1. Include a greeting, close and a signature unless you are sure you do not need them.

2. If you are not sure whether you should be formal or informal, lean towards being formal.

3. Keep your signature brief. A maximum of four lines is reasonable.

4. If your e-mail system allows you to include a signature automatically, use it. You may have different signatures for different purposes such as for work and personal messages.

5. Include a disclaimer, copyright or other notice as appropriate.

purpose, timing and content

1. Avoid sending very long messages (for example more than 100 lines).

2. Be clear about the purpose of your message. If necessary, make your purpose known early in your message. Also, avoid having more than one purpose.

3. If the recipient does not know you, introduce yourself early in your message.

4. If the message contains material that is someone else's work, make it clear in your message and give full credit to the original author. If the material is under copyright, obtain permission before using it.

5. Reply to messages for which a reply is expected, even if the purpose is politely to withdraw from any future communication.

6. Reply to messages in an appropriate timeframe.

7. Allow a reasonable amount of time before sending follow-up messages which may suggest that your original message did not arrive or that the recipient is not responding.

8. If a message contains an earlier message (for example, if you are replying to a message), check whether it needs to be included and delete it if it does not.

9. If you want to be sure that your message has been received, ask the recipient to send you a brief acknowledgement, even if they respond in full to your message later.

style and format

1. The body of your message should have a beginning, middle and end (unless it is a short message).

2. Write your message clearly (in plain language).

3. Make sure the content is appropriate to all the recipients, not just a subset of them.

4. Check your spelling, grammar, punctuation and readability. You may be able to set up your e-mail system so that it automatically checks the spelling before it sends a message.

5. Do not write messages only in block capitals or lower case text. Use mixed (sentence) case.

6. Do not use abbreviations, slang, humour or sarcasm unless you are sure the recipient will understand them.

7. If you use symbols or special characters, beware that they might look different to the recipient.

8. If you use smileys and other emoticons to indicate tone, use them sparingly.

9. Remember that the meaning of words and phrases may vary from country to country, and that the format of information (such as dates) may also be different.

10. If you provide any information in a message, check that it is correct. If necessary be explicit about what is opinion, what is fact and what is supposition.

11. If your e-mail system's text editor does not have a word wrap facility, keep your line length to less than 80 characters (say about 75 characters to be safe).

security

1. Protect any sensitive information you send by e-mail.

2. Keep a copy of important messages. If you keep a copy of messages, you may need to protect them if they contain any sensitive information.

3. Check your PC's date and time whenever you log on to your e-mail system.

4. Change your e-mail system password regularly (at least every month).

5. Do not give your e-mail UserId or password to anyone.

attachments

1. Do not attach files unless they are necessary.

2. Before you send an attachment check that the person you are sending it to will be able to access it. For example, you should check that they have the right software and, if necessary, the right version of the software.

3. Limit the number of files that you attach to messages (no more than five files and ideally just one or two).

4. Limit the size of files that you attach to messages (the total size of all attachments to a message should be no more than 500Kb). On internal messages consider placing the attachment on a shared (file server) directory and include the location of the file in your message.

5. Compress large files that you attach. If you compress a file, before you send it you should check that the recipient will be able to expand it.

6. If your attachment contains sensitive information, protect it appropriately.

7. If you forward a message that you receive which has an attached file, check that the attached file does not contain a virus.

8. If you reply to a message that has an attachment, do not return the attachment with your reply.

message checklist

Here are some questions that you can ask yourself about the messages you send.

1. Am I sending the message to the right person? If I chose the person from a list in my e-mail system, am I sure I have chosen the right person?

2. Is my message important? If so, have I put an appropriate label in the subject line?

3. Is the purpose of my message clear?

4. Is the subject line clear?

5. Is my message well structured and written clearly?

6. Does my message contain anything that is illegal, anything which could offend or harm someone or could be damaging or annoying?

7. Have I checked the spelling and grammar?

8. Do I expect a reply (or other action)? If so, have I said so and have I requested a timescale?

9. Does the message contain any sensitive information? If so, should I really send it by e-mail? If so, have I protected it and have I asked the person to whom I am sending it to confirm when they receive it?

10. Do I need to include a disclaimer, copyright notice or other notice?

11. Does the message contain previous e-mails? If so, do they also need to be included as part of the e-mail or can I delete them?

12. Is there an attachment? If so:

- Have I protected any sensitive information?

- Does the person I am sending it to have the right software to be able to read it?

- Have I actually included (or 'attached') it?

summary

The key point of this chapter is to apply common sense when writing messages.

You might think that the chapter includes nothing that is not obvious – and you would be right. However, every day hundreds of thousands of business messages are sent and received which fall short of at least one of the six characteristics introduced at the beginning of the chapter. This does not necessarily mean that they are all bad messages, but it does mean that they could be better.

The best practice guidelines are what they say they are – 'guidelines'. They are not rules to be applied blindly and there is no guarantee that you will suffer if you do not always follow them.

Good messages are written for the recipient. They are not intended to be clever, just effective.

appendices

➤ **at a glance**

finding someone's e-mail address

public key infrastructure explained

example business e-mail policy statements

example disclaimer and confidentiality noticies

appendix A

finding someone's e-mail address

How can you find out someone's business e-mail address? In general there are four things that you can do.

1. *Contact them in another way.*

   Direct contact (such as phoning them) can be the most effective way of getting an e-mail address.

2. *Send a message to their company's Postmaster*

   (e.g. postmaster@ourcompany.com).

   The e-mail service should have implemented the role of Postmaster.

3. *Go to their company web site* (if they have one).

   Many company web sites include e-mail addresses of useful contacts who may be able to help you.

4. *Use an Internet directory service.*

   There are many directory services available on the web including those listed in the Table A.1.

Directory name	Web address
The E-Mail Address Book	www.emailbook.com
The World Email Directory	www.worldemail.com
Bigfoot	www.bigfoot.com
Four11	www.four11.com
Switchboard	www.switchboard.com
WhoWhere	www.whowhere.com

Table A.1
Directory services
for e-mail
addresses

Some of the search engines (for example, Yahoo!, Netscape, Lycos and NetFind) provide access to directory services to find e-mail addresses and so do some e-mail systems (such as Microsoft® Outlook® and Netscape® Communicator®).

It will always help to have as much information as you can get about the person you want to find. Many of the search engines allow you to enter additional, qualifying details to limit the results returned.

In general you should not try guessing what the address might be (the possible consequences of sending a message to the wrong person are obvious).

> ▶▶▶ **WATCH POINT** You should not distribute someone else's e-mail address without their permission.

appendix B

public key infrastructure explained

This section takes a closer look at public key infrastructure (PKI) and is structured as follows:

- public and private key pairs
- certificates and certificate authorities
- certificate revocation lists
- digital signatures.

public and private key pairs

PKI is based on an encryption method (or algorithm) which uses 'keys' to encrypt and decrypt messages. There is a private key that typically is a pair of large prime numbers. The product of those two numbers is the public key.

Consider a user, say, Adam. Adam generates a private and public key pair – either the software that comes as part of the security system he is using on the PC generates it on his behalf; or he goes to an external agency, such as Verisign, which generates it on his behalf (for a small fee) – and lists the public key in a public directory. A second user, Bettie, can then use that public key to encrypt a message she wants to send to Adam. Adam's software can use his knowledge of the two original prime numbers to decrypt the message.

Even if a third person, say Eve, saw the encrypted message to Adam and knew Adam's public key, she would still have the mammoth task of splitting the public key into its two prime numbers before she could decode the message. The longer the numbers, the longer this will take. The length of the numbers is usually measured in terms of the number of bits. A competent computer science graduate could probably crack a 40-bit code over the weekend using one or two machines in his university. Most government security services could probably crack a 56-bit code in under an hour. But because even the CIA cannot normally crack a 128-bit code in a useful timeframe, the US government has classified such codes as armaments and has restricted their export.

>>> **INFO POINT** A 128-bit number is a number between 1 and 340,282,366,920,900,000,000,000,000,000,000,000,000.

In binary an example of such a number is:

10010111010110001101101010000110101000101011110101010 00001000110011100111100101101011110101010101011000111101 11001110011101000110.

One of the problems with PKI is that it is computationally very slow; that is, when you hit the 'encrypt' button on your PC it can take a while to process it.

An alternative approach is to combine it with a symmetric key system such as the Data Encryption Standard (DES). (In a symmetric key system the sender and receiver both use the same key to encrypt and decrypt.) PKI is used as the basic trust mechanism. This is used to establish a secure communication between any sender and any recipient. Once that communication channel has been set up, the sender can generate a new DES key which he sends to the recipient and they both use that key just for the duration of that session.

Applying this to your messages – the first part of the message contains this 'one time' DES key which itself is encrypted using the recipient's public key. The main text of the message is then encrypted with the DES key. There are now a number of e-mail products working to this combined approach using PKI, and then using that connection to exchange a symmetric DES key for the actual message. While this technology is necessary to achieve fast, effective security, the operation of it should be transparent to the user.

If Adam and Bettie want to use public/private key pairs to protect their messages from Eve, or any other Tom, Dick or Harry, then those key pairs are really all they need. But if the technology is to be used on a wider scale then you need a trusted way of linking individuals to their public keys. This is what the infrastructure in PKI is all about. The main components of this are:

- certificates and certificate authorities
- certificate revocation lists
- digital signatures.

These are discussed in the following sections.

certificates and certificate authorities

A digital certificate contains a public key and enough details to identify the owner of the certificate.

The certificates will normally be stored in a directory. So as long as you trust the certificate, you can use the public key to send secure messages to the owner of the certificate. By analogy, you trust the phone company to produce an accurate directory of phone numbers. So you can look up an individual in the directory, get his number and if you call that number, you have a reasonable degree of certainty that the call will go through to him and nobody else.

The role of a certificate authority (CA) is to act as a trusted organization that will issue certificates and maintain a directory linking certificates to individuals. Everybody who trusts that CA can then use its directory to get, say, Adam's public key and then use that public key to encrypt a message to Adam.

However, just as you might have difficulty convincing a US policeman that your UK driving licence was valid, so you might not trust the certificates issued by a certificate authority. There are proposals to set up a global network of trusted CAs. As yet nothing has been agreed, but then consider that it has taken over thirty years for countries in the European Community to agree a common driving licence. A certificate is only as good as the authority that issued it, and as yet there is no legal reason why you should not set up your own CA and issue yourself with a certificate with the name William Clinton and an address in Pennsylvania Avenue. Until such time as we have a global network of trusted CAs, then it is very much up to the individual to understand what checks a CA has undertaken before he places any reliance on a digital certificate.

certificate revocation lists

When you are using a credit card to buy goods in a shop, the shop wants to be sure that the card is valid before they give you the goods. They can check that the card looks genuine, but this does not protect them from people using stolen cards. To do so they need some method of checking with the card issuing authority that the card has not been revoked for one reason or another.

The simplest way of doing this is for the card issuer to publish a daily or weekly 'hot card' list of cards that have been reported stolen. In exactly the same way, a certificate authority should publish a list of certificates that may have been stolen or otherwise compromised. This is known as a certificate revocation list (so that it can have another TLA, namely CRL). But there is still no legal requirement for a CA to publish a CRL, let alone publish an up-to-date one. What is even worse is that while some e-mail systems say they support PKI, they do not provide any support for checking CRLs.

Just as the credit card industry is moving from 'hot card' lists to on-line checking, so too PKI is moving to on-line certificate status processing (OCSP). But the standards have yet to be agreed (perhaps because it is not a TLA!) and products are only just coming on the market.

digital signatures

The concept of a digital signature is to give e-mail messages a similar standing as a pen-and-ink signature gives to paper documents. Digital signatures are relatively new and they have the potential to add a new level of security to e-mail and other electronic media.

An ink signature on the bottom of a document actually proves little more than the fact that you have signed the document. The courts will normally make the assumption that you have read the document and that the text has not been changed since you signed it.

A life assurance scam centred on the fact that a dishonest salesman presented an unsuspecting client with four copies of a policy to sign, rather than the usual two. The bottom two contained a 'deliberate error' in that the value of the policy was increased tenfold, by the addition of an extra '0'. Short of going through each document line by line, the customer had no means of knowing that the last two documents were different from the first.

Computers are ideally suited to this type of checking. The standard technique is to convert letters to numbers and use a simple mathematical formula to calculate a single large number that represents the text. This function is known as a hash function. The computer can use the same hash function to compare two versions of the same document – if the hash function produces the same hash value then we assume the documents are identical. In the past this has been used to check for accidental errors, perhaps caused by hardware problems. But the same techniques can be applied to check whether or not a document has been tampered with.

Once Adam has written his letter to Bettie, he can use a standard hash function, such as Message Digest Three (MD3), to create a hash value for the message. Adam can then use his private key to encrypt the hash value and send both the original message and the encrypted hash value to Bettie. She can use Adam's public key to decrypt the hash value and compare this with the value she obtains by applying the hash function to the text of the message she has received. If the two are the same, then Bettie can be sure that Eve has not tampered with the message after Adam signed it.

On top of all this, Adam could use Bettie's public key to encrypt the whole message text and hash value to stop Eve even reading the message. It is important to realize that this gives us two ways in which we can use public keys: one for ensuring the confidentiality of documents; the other to ensure the accuracy of documents. The solution is for the software to select either the sender's or recipient's key pair depending on whether signature or confidentiality (or both) is required. As you might expect, not all software products support this option.

appendix C

example business e-mail policy statements

Here are three examples of e-mail policies. They are included for illustrative purposes only and are not intended to be model examples.

> **▶▶▶ WATCH POINT** If you are in any doubt about the contents of your company policy, you should get professional advice. For example, you should consider input from HR, legal and possibly other experts.

example 1

The purpose of this policy is to ensure the proper use of OurCompany's e-mail system by its employees. E-mail is a tool for business communication and users have the responsibility to use this resource in an efficient, effective, ethical and lawful manner. E-mail communications should follow the same standards expected in written business communications and public meetings. Violation of this policy may result in disciplinary action, including possible termination and/or legal action.

All e-mail accounts maintained on the e-mail systems are the sole property of OurCompany. OurCompany has the right to monitor any employee's e-mail account for legitimate business reasons, including compliance with this policy, employee performance and where there is reasonable suspicion of activities that violate this policy.

The following use of the e-mail system is strictly prohibited. Users receiving such material should immediately report the incident to the appropriate authority.

- The creation and exchange of messages that are offensive, harassing, obscene or threatening.

- The exchange of propriety information, trade secrets or any other privileged, confidential or sensitive information. Caution should be taken to ensure that messages are addressed to the appropriate recipient; it is easy inadvertently to address e-mail messages incorrectly. Confidential messages should include a warning regarding accidental transmission to an unintended third party.

- The creation and exchange of advertisements, solicitations, chain letters and other unsolicited e-mail. The creation and exchange of information in violation of any copyright laws.

- Registration to list servers without proper authorization. Subscription to such a service can result in an overload of received messages directly impacting the performance of the e-mail system.

- Forwarding messages to another person without the permission of the originator.

- Messages should not be read or sent from another user's account except under proper delegate arrangements.

- Altering or copying a message or attachment belonging to another user without the permission of the originator.

- Users must not compromise the privacy of their password by giving it to others or exposing it to public view. Passwords should be changed on a regular basis.

- Retain messages only if relevant to the business or anticipated litigation. Messages will be retained by the e-mail system for not more than 60 days.

- Address messages to recipients who need to know rather than to everyone you know. Messages sent unnecessarily can impact system and user performance.

- Construct messages professionally (spelling, grammar) and efficiently (subject filed, attachments).

- Incidental personal use of the e-mail system is not acceptable.

example 2

1 introduction

While staff are encouraged to use the electronic mail messaging (e-mail) facility in the course of their work, OurCompany's assets must not be misused. To distribute or obtain offensive, abusive, obscene, racist, sexist, or otherwise unlawful material falls into this category of misuse.

The distribution/access/storage of offensive and/or non-business material is not an acceptable use of OurCompany's assets. Misuse of OurCompany's communication systems is regarded as misconduct, which may result in disciplinary action being taken against the offending individual and may even lead to dismissal.

2 general

Each member of staff is required to comply with OurCompany's Electronic Mail Messaging Policy. OurCompany reserves the right at its discretion to amend, suspend or withdraw any section or part of this policy by way of individual or general notice, to take immediate effect.

3 personal use

Electronic mail is a privilege and should be used responsibly. The main purpose for providing electronic mail at OurCompany is for business activities. Responsible personal use is permitted, provided that it is reasonable and:

- is not likely to cause the Company loss
- is not for personal gain
- does not constitute a solicitation
- does not contravene any of OurCompany's policies and guidelines
- is not detrimental to OurCompany's image
- does not interfere with work.

If staff are unsure about the material they wish to send, or are concerned about any material which they may have received, they must discuss this with their immediate manager.

Issues of confidentiality, copyright and data/information protection must be discussed with OurCompany's Information Protection Manager.

Any of the following examples of mail usage are strictly prohibited and are subject to normal Human Resources disciplinary procedures:

- Forgery (or attempted forgery) of electronic mail messages.
- Attempts to read, delete, copy, or modify the electronic mail of other users.
- Attempts at sending harassing, obscene and/or other threatening e-mail to another user.
- Attempts at sending unsolicited junk e-mail, 'for-profit' messages or chain letters.
- Attempts to intercept other users' e-mail.

This list is by way of illustration and is by no means exhaustive.

4 system monitoring

E-mail usage in OurCompany is monitored by the Information Systems Department. This includes ensuring the delivery of messages internally and to/from the Internet. Never assume that your e-mail cannot be read by anyone else; others may be able to read or access your mail. However, user files and mail are intended to be private. The user's files will be examined only when authorized by an appropriate Human Resources Manager within OurCompany, as part of an audit and/or investigations.

5 e-mail accounts

Only the user's account/mailbox should be used on the mail system. Passwords should not be given to other people and should be changed frequently. Passwords must not be written down, or used in any other processes that facilitate automatic log-ons. The mailbox owners are responsible and are liable for all messages sent from their e-mail accounts. E-mail accounts are to be used only by the authorized owner of the account for the authorized purpose. Users may not share their account name or password with another person. Account owners are ultimately responsible for all activity performed under their account. The only exceptions to the above are secretarial functions that have responsibilities for their managers' e-mail, or where the manager has given permission for a member of their team to use another team member's e-mail account.

6 legal requirements

Any message sent or received via OurCompany's e-mail system, like any OurCompany communication, may be monitored by OurCompany at any time, without prior notification. If OurCompany discovers anything construed as misconduct or criminal activity, the information contained in such e-mail messages may be used to document such conduct. These may be revealed to the appropriate authorities, both internally and externally to OurCompany. Do not write or keep anything that you would not send in a formal letter, or mention in conversation. E-mails sent to customers or third party suppliers may be construed as legally binding. It is accepted that e-mails carry the authority of the sender.

7 disclaimer

The following message is to be inserted into all external e-mails:

Internet communications are not secure and therefore OurCompany does not accept legal responsibility for the contents of this message. Any views or opinions presented are solely those of the author and do not necessarily represent those of OurCompany.

8 dormant accounts

E-mail accounts not used for sixty (60) consecutive days will be deactivated and deleted.

9 leavers

Upon notification from HR and/or the user's immediate manager/supervisor, a leaver's e-mail account will be deactivated with immediate effect.

10 housekeeping

Users should delete all messages from the mail system when they are no longer needed, as a finite amount of storage space is available for electronic mail. Any messages which users want to keep should be saved onto their own hard drive or floppy disk. Messages will automatically be deleted after a specified amount of time. Prior to the removal of aged mail, all users will be notified with the message: 'your message file size has exceeded the site standard', giving the user the opportunity to 'housekeep'. Once messages are removed/deleted, they cannot be restored/recovered.

11 mail standards

The following are a sample of standards and best practices, which should be adhered to:

● Do not overuse e-mail by sending courtesy copies of messages to people who do not need them. Similarly, it is not generally necessary to reply to an e-mail just to inform the sender that you have received it.

● Be careful when forwarding e-mail messages. Use common sense; if you would not forward a paper copy of a memo with the same information, do not forward the e-mail.

● Be careful what you write. E-mail is not the same as conversation. It is a written record and can be duplicated freely.

● Use normal capitalization and punctuation. Typing a message in all capitals is bad etiquette.

● When replying to e-mail, it is often useful to include a portion of the original sender's message to put your reply into context. It is appropriate to delete unimportant portions of the original message in order to prevent the message from getting too long.

● Imported software and files must be scanned for viruses before being opened.

OurCompany reserves the right to suspend any e-mail account it believes has been inappropriately used.

example 3

risks

E-mail is a quick, easy and flexible way of communicating. It is an effective way of sharing information and it is used to discuss and deal with many business issues.

Because e-mail is easy to use, the risks associated with using it are often overlooked. Here are some of those risks.

- People can read or change messages you are sending.
- People can read, change or delete messages you have stored.
- People can change the direction of messages you are sending.
- It may be impossible to find out who sent a message, especially if it is passed on by many people.
- Items sent as attachments (or enclosures) to messages may contain viruses or other harmful codes.
- You cannot be sure that the person you are sending the message to actually receives it.
- Messages may be sent which are intended to cause disruption, for example 'chain mail' and hoax virus messages.

standards

E-mail is a business tool. You should treat it like you would any other business tool (such as the phone). It is not free, it is not confidential and, like any computer system, it is not totally reliable.

Please remember the following standards when you use our e-mail systems.

- Do not send an e-mail to someone to whom you would not send a letter.
- Only send messages to people who need to receive them – do not copy them unnecessarily.
- Do not write something in an e-mail that you would not write in a letter or say to someone's face.

- Do not send an e-mail to someone by using another member of staff's e-mail UserId and password.

- E-mail messages must not contain material which is illegal or which could offend or harm anyone (such as insulting, sexist or racist material). If you receive a message which contains this type of material (either as part of the message or as an attachment), tell your line manager as soon as possible and keep it as evidence. You must not pass it on to anyone else.

  If you send a message which contains this type of material (either as part of the message or as an attachment), OurCompany has the right to take disciplinary action against you.

- Do not use e-mail to enter into a contract, or change or end an existing contract with an organization which is not part of OurCompany.

- Any secret or restricted information you send by e-mail must be protected. (See 'Protecting information' below.)

- Keep your e-mail password confidential.

- You must follow our published policies and standards. (These include policies covering discrimination, harassment, security and the Data Protection Act.)

- OurCompany can inspect any message which is sent or received by its e-mail systems.
- Misuse of the e-mail systems *may* result in disciplinary action.

protecting information

Secret information is information which would cause serious damage to us if it was made public. Some examples of secret information are:

- plans to change our structure significantly (such as merger or takeover plans)

- information about our shares (such as share 'buyback' or 'new share issues')

- information which would allow someone to break our security precautions (such as office alarm codes).

Restricted information is information which would cause harm or embarrassment to us if it was made public. Some examples of restricted information are:

- details of a new product or service that OurCompany is developing

- information about a customer which could significantly embarrass them (such as financial difficulties)

- plans which include named redundancies or promotions.

Unclassified information is the vast majority of the information we use on a day-to-day basis. It is normally still confidential and it includes customer information.

You must treat unclassified information with care and only share it with people who need to see it.

- Any secret or restricted information you send by e-mail *must* be protected. One way that you can do this is by putting the information in an attachment (such as a Microsoft® Word® or Excel® file) and protecting the file with a password. Use another method (such as the phone) to give the password to the person you want to receive the information.

  Warning: If you protect a Microsoft® Word® or Excel® file with a password and then forget the password, you will not be able to open the file, access the information in it or remove the password protection. You should consider keeping a list of passwords. If you do this, make sure you keep the list in a safe place.

- Any stored e-mail messages which contain secret or restricted information *must* be protected. You can do this in two ways.

— Put the information in an attachment (in the same way as when you send an e-mail which contains secret or restricted information).

— Store the information on a network and use the network security to prevent people from entering the area where the information is stored.

● If you send a message to another member of staff, do not copy it to anyone outside OurCompany. If you need to send a message to someone who is not a member of staff you should write a separate message (and you can copy it to OurCompany staff if you need to).

best practice for e-mails

security and control

● Do not rely on the e-mail system to store messages over a long period of time. If you want to keep messages for a long time, you should save them in a file storage system (for example, like you save word-processing files).

● E-mail messages may be used as evidence in a court of law. Therefore you should consider how long you need to keep your messages. If your messages are to do with a legal dispute, you should print them and keep the print in a safe place.

● Use software to detect viruses on your workstation or PC so that when you open an attachment, it is automatically checked for viruses. (Refer to your IT unit for more information on how to detect viruses.)

● If your workstation or PC is logged into an e-mail system and you leave it unattended, you should switch on your password protected screen saver if you have one.

housekeeping

● Change your e-mail password at least once a month.

● Change you screen saver password at least once a month.

● At least once a week delete any saved messages you no longer need which you have stored in folders or left in your 'in basket'. (Also, if your e-mail system has a 'wastebasket' function, set it to be emptied automatically when you exit the e-mail system.) You can save e-mail messages as text files and store them with your other files.

- If your e-mail system has a 'personal address book' feature, do not rely on it. (Addresses in personal address books are not updated automatically if they change.)

- Do not send an e-mail message to more than fifty people. You should ask your IT unit how the message should be sent.

timing, style and content

- Reply soon to messages, especially if they are sent by our customers.

- E-mail messages should have a structure (such as a beginning, middle and an end – just like a letter).

- Do not write messages in block capitals as they can seem aggressive.

- Check the spellings. (You may be able to set up your workstation or PC so that it automatically checks the spelling before it sends a message.)

- If an e-mail contains messages which have been sent in the past, check if they need to be included as part of the e-mail. Delete them if they do not need to be included.

- If your message is important you should label it in line with this.

attachments

- Do not use attachments unnecessarily. Attachments to e-mails can increase the size of the information that is sent over our networks. This can make our networks less efficient.

- Before you open or copy a file that is attached to an e-mail from outside OurCompany, check that it does not contain a virus. (Many workstations and PCs now include software which automatically scans attachments for viruses when you try to open them. If you are not sure if your workstations or PC has this software, you should contact your IT unit.)

- Check the level of security you need for files which you attach and use the appropriate security measures.

- Do not keep attachments in the e-mail system. Save them with your other files (such as your word-processing files). Also, do not leave messages in the e-mail system just because you want to keep the attachments.

- Compress large attachments. That is, use software to reduce the size of large attachments. As a guide, if an attachment is 300K or larger, you should compress it. If you need advice on how to compress and expand files, contact your IT unit.

- Before you send an attachment check that the person you are sending it to will be able to read it. For example, you should check that they have the right software and, if necessary, the right version of the software. If you compressed the file before you sent it, you should check that they will be able to expand it.

If you have any questions about how to use our E-mail systems you should contact your IT unit.

appendix D

example disclaimer and confidentiality notices

Here is a selection of disclaimer and confidentiality notices. They are included for illustrative purposes only and are not intended to be model examples.

a law firm

This email and any files transmitted with it are confidential and intended solely for the use of the individual or entity to whom they are addressed. If you have received this email in error please notify the system manager.

This footnote also confirms that this email message has been swept by MIMEsweeper for the presence of computer viruses.

www.mimesweeper.com

a utility company

NOTE: This E-mail is private and confidential to the named recipients. Any information provided is given in good faith. However, unless specifically stated to the contrary, OurCompany accepts no liability for the content of this E-mail, or for the consequences of any actions taken on the basis of the information provided, unless that information is subsequently confirmed in writing. The unauthorised copying of any information contained in this E-mail to persons other than the named recipients is strictly forbidden.

a bank

The contents of this e-mail may be privileged and are confidential. It may not be disclosed to or used by anyone other than the addressee(s), nor copied in any way. If received in error, please advise the sender, then delete it from your system.

OurCompany Registered Number 999999 England. Registered Office: OurOffices, TheTown, TheCounty Regulated by the Personal Investment Authority and IMRO for investment business. Member of OurCompany Group, advising on the life assurance, pensions and unit trust products only of that Group.

a global technology advisory firm

CONFIDENTIALITY/PROPRIETARY NOTE

The document accompanying this transmission contains information from OurCompany, Inc. which is confidential, proprietary or copyrighted and is intended solely for the use of the individual or entity named on this transmission. If you are not the intended recipient, you are notified that disclosing, copying, distributing or taking any action in reliance on the contents of this information is strictly prohibited. This prohibition, includes, without limitation, displaying this transmission, or any portion thereof, on any public bulletin board. If you are not the intended recipient of this document, this document should be returned to OurCompany, Inc. immediately. Please contact OurCompany so that we can arrange for the return of this transmission to us at no cost to you.

a security firm

DISCLAIMER

Any opinions expressed in this email are those of the individual and not necessarily the Company. This email and any files transmitted with it, including replies and forwarded copies (which may contain alterations) subsequently transmitted from the Company, are confidential and solely for the use of the intended recipient. It may contain material protected by attorney-client privilege. If you are not the intended recipient or the person responsible for delivering to the intended recipient, be advised that you have received this email in error and that any use is strictly prohibited.

If you have received this email in error please notify the IT manager by telephone on 123 456 7890 or via email to OurCompany, including a copy of this message. Please then delete this email and destroy any copies of it.

a healthcare company

Internet communications are not secure and therefore OurCompany does not accept legal responsibility for the contents of this message. Any views or opinions presented are solely those of the author and do not necessarily represent those of OurCompany.

glossary

address book   A facility of many e-mail systems to store and manage e-mail addresses (and often other contact information such as full name, company details and so on).

anonymous remailer   When you send a message via an anonymous remailer, it removes the identity of the sender, inserts an alias (which is randomly generated) and forwards the message to the intended recipient.

application   A particular role or task that you can ask a computer to do, or more usually, the software used for that purpose.

asymmetric encryption   Encrypting and decrypting computer information by using a pair of 'keys', one of which is public and the other is private. The public key is freely available and is used to encrypt messages, the private key is known only to the recipient and is used to decrypt the message. See also *encryption* and *symmetric encryption*.

attachment   A file added to an e-mail message so that it may be sent through the e-mail system. See also *MIME*.

authentication   The verification of the identity of a person or process. Authentication verifies that an e-mail message really has come from the stated source.

bandwidth   The capacity of a telecommunications component such as a phone line. Usually expressed as a number of bits or kilo-bits transmitted per second.

browser   Software used to access the Internet and the World Wide Web.

bulletin board   A computer and associated software which provides an electronic message database where people can log in and leave messages. Messages are usually split into topic groups.

certificate (digital)   A digital certificate is a token issued by a trusted party to guarantee the authenticity of a message. See also *authentication*.

chat (room)   A system that enables users to have an interactive (real-time) typed conversation. What you type on your PC is seen at the same time by the person or people you are communicating with, and vice versa.

client   As part of the client/server pair, the client is the software item that requests information or services from a *server*. The machine (usually a PC) on which the software runs is often incorporated in the description of client. See also *server*.

compression (algorithm) software   Software used to reduce the size of a file. See also *decompression*.

decompression (algorithm) software   Software used to expand a compressed file to its original size. See also *compression*.

DES   Data Encryption Standard. The most widely used standard for symmetric encryption. See also *symmetric encryption*.

digital certificate   See *certificate*.

digital signature   See *signature*.

distribution list (group)   A named group of e-mail addresses. You can send a message to all of the addresses in the group by referring only to the group name.

domain (name)   The part of an e-mail address which follows the @ sign. It is a name that uniquely identifies a computer on a network. In the e-mail address 'hostmaster@ourcompany.com' the domain name is 'ourcompany.com'.

download   The transfer of a computer file from a server to a PC (client). See also *upload*.

EDI   Electronic Data Interchange. The exchange of business documents between computers using agreed standards. Often used for the exchange of information between trading partners.

e-mail   Electronic mail. The transfer of messages between computers attached to a network.

e-mail system   The client and server software that collectively provide the capability to create, send, retrieve and manage electronic messages.

emoticon   Emotional icon. Characters added to messages to convey emotions such as 'humour', for example, a 'smiley' ☺ .

encryption   A security process that 'scrambles' computer information so that it can only be unscrambled by someone who has an appropriate de-scrambler (or key). See also *asymmetric encryption* and *asymmetric encryption*.

executable   A file containing software which is ready to be run (or executed).

extranet   An *Intranet* that has been extended so that some or all of its content is accessible to selected external parties.

filter   Software that can examine incoming and outgoing messages (including their addresses, subject lines, content and attachments) and takes actions depending upon rules defined to it.

firewall   A combination of hardware and software that acts as a security boundary between parts of a network. Often used by companies to provide 'safe' access between their private networks and the public Internet. Firewalls act at a network level; they do not consider the content of messages. See also *filter*.

flame   A 'heated' (that is, aggressive) e-mail message.

folder   A named subdivision of a computer disk into which files can be stored.

groupware   Groupware is a set of technology tools that lets businesses share information. Examples include scheduling and database facilities.

HTML   Hypertext Mark-up Language. The computer language used to create the pages that make up the World Wide Web.

hyperlink (hypertext)   Most commonly found on web pages, they are objects such as text or images which, when you click on them, enable you to jump to other web pages. Hyperlinks can also be used in e-mail messages, for example to include the address of your company's web site. See also *plain text*.

IMAP4   Internet Message Access Protocol (Version 4) is a standard for receiving e-mail. It is a client/server protocol where only message headers are downloaded from the server to the client, reducing the time taken to identify messages that are worth reading. The full message is retrieved if the user decides to read it. All e-mails are stored on the server until the user removes them. See also *POP3*.

internet   The global network of computers. It uses the Internet Protocol (IP) as a communication standard.

intranet   An internal Internet which provides all the benefits of Internet technology with the added benefit of reliability and security. It uses the same technology (browsers, web servers, TCP/IP, HTML, etc.) but is confined to private (company) networks.

ISP   Internet Service Provider. A company that provides Internet services including high bandwidth connectivity to the Internet, e-mail and web hosting facilities. An ISP will have their own high bandwidth network services connected to the Internet.

junk mail   See *spam*.

list server   See *mailing list*.

mailing list   A server which copies mail on a particular topic to all those users who have subscribed to that topic.

MIME   Multipurpose Internet Mail Extensions. This defines the standard representation for messages that do not conform to a straightforward ASCII representation. For example, a word-processed document. MIME is used to transmit attachments to e-mail messages.

modem   Modulator/demodulator. A device that enables computer-based information to be transmitted over an analogue phone network.

newsgroup   A newsgroup is an electronic discussion group, organized by topic. You can subscribe and send messages on any of the topics and view the contributions of others.

off-line   In an off-line state the client (PC) is not connected to the service provider's server and so messages cannot be sent or received. (Some e-mail systems allow you to create messages off-line.) See also *on-line*.

on-line   In an on-line state the client (PC) is connected to the service provider's server and so messages can be sent and received. See also *off-line*.

operating system   Base layer of software that interfaces and controls the hardware components and the processes that run on them.

PDA   Personal Digital Assistant. A small, handheld computer designed to perform everyday tasks such as letter writing and scheduling meetings. PDAs are also being used to access the World Wide Web and to send and receive e-mails.

PDF   Portable Data Format. The file format for Adobe Systems' Acrobat. PDF is a file format for representing documents in a manner that is independent of the original application software, hardware and operating system.

PGP   Pretty Good Privacy. A high security public key encryption application for a variety of computer platforms (operating systems).

PKI   Public key infrastructure (PKI) is a collection of components which provides a secure method of communication, including the use of public and private keys to encrypt and decrypt e-mail messages. See also *authentication, certificate (digital), encryption, signature (digital)*.

plain text   Text that contains no embedded format or layout information, or encryption. See also *hyperlink (hypertext)*.

POP   Point-of-Presence. The point at which a client connects to an ISP's server. This is the ISP's phone number that you call to make a dial-in connection.

POP3   Post Office Protocol (Version 3). The most common Internet standard for e-mail. When you use POP3, all new messages are downloaded from the server at once whenever you check your e-mail. See also *IMAP4*.

protocol   The set of rules that define how computer systems should communicate across a network.

RSA   A type of encryption algorithm named after the inventors: Rivest, Shamir and Adleman.

RTF   Rich Text Format. A standard machine readable text format supported by some e-mail systems.

self-extracting file   A file which has been compressed and which contains the software necessary to decompress it. See also *compression* and *decompression*.

server   As part of the client/server pair, the server is the software item that delivers information or services to *clients*. The machine (usually a medium or large computer) on which the software runs is often incorporated in the description of server. See also *client*.

signature (digital)   Information appended to a message that identifies the sender and confirms that the message is complete (unaltered).

SLA   Service Level Agreement. A contract between a service supplier and a service receiver which states the level of service that the supplier will provide.

smiley   ☺ See *emoticon*.

S-MIME   Secure-Multipurpose Internet Mail Extensions (*MIME*). An extension to MIME which adds security features (encryption and authentication). See also *MIME*.

SMS   Short Message Service. A protocol used in mobile phone communications for sending and receiving short (160 characters) text messages.

SMTP Simple Mail Transport Protocol. A protocol used to send and receive e-mail messages, especially between e-mail servers.

spam Junk e-mail. Also referred to as 'unsolicited commercial e-mail' and sometimes 'unsolicited bulk e-mail'.

speech recognition The generation of text from speech (sound).

speech synthesis The generation of speech (sound) from text.

symmetric encryption Encrypting and decrypting computer information by using a single 'key' which is shared by the sender and the recipient to encrypt and decrypt the message respectively. See also *Asymmetric encryption* and *encryption*.

system See *e-mail system*.

system administrator A person responsible for the management and configuration of the e-mail system.

TCP/IP Transmission Control Protocol over Internet Protocol. The de facto network standard for Internet communication.

text editor A basic word processor that forms a part of the e-mail system.

TTS Text-to-Speech. See *speech synthesis*.

unified messaging The amalgamation of separate message formats (text, voice and image) using standard protocols.

upload The transfer of a computer file from a PC (client) to a server. See also *download*.

URL Uniform Resource Locator. A unique address which points to an Internet resource, such as a web page.

virus A computer program that has the ability to self-replicate and spread to other computers and which is designed to be annoying or destructive.

WAP Wireless Application Protocol. A set of standards for wireless communication between systems, for example, accessing the Internet from a mobile phone.

web-based e-mail   E-mail that does not require specific e-mail software but uses the facilities of a standard web browser interacting with a specialist e-mail web site.

workflow   Workflow relates to the automation of business processes. It allows a business to use tools accurately to describe their business processes in terms of tasks, policies, skills and service levels. The tools then support the processes by capturing, distributing, managing and monitoring work items according to the rules defined for the processes.

world wide web (the web)   The vast store of information accessed using the Internet.

index

accessibility 30–1
  unauthorized access 74, 80–1
accounts 59, 174–5
acknowledgement of receipt 76, 155–6
address
  choice 58–9
  finding 164–5
  lists 60
Address Book 26, 60
  definition 187
  update 69
addresses, address lists, distribution lists
    58–61
  address lists 60
  choice of e–mail address 58–9
  distribution lists 61
addressing messages 142–4
  address lines 142–3
  subject line 143–4
addressing and subject lines 158
affordability 3
aggressive materials 19
Alexander Forbes Risk Services 94, 136
Allsops 32
Anonymous re–mailing 72
  definition 187
anti-virus software 19, 79
application, definition 187
archiving 54–6
  definition 54
  security 87
asymmetric encryption, definition 187

attachments 4, 26, 32–4, 61–2, 160–1,
    181–2
  definition 187
  format 152
  name 150
  number 151–2
  protection 152
  security 85–6
  size 150–1
  storing 54
  to messages 148–52
  type 149–50
authentication 74, 77, 88
  definition 187
  sender 77
auto-management facilities 63–4
auto-reply 69

backing up 54–6, 69
  definition 54
bandwidth, definition 187
benefits 120–1
best practice 180–2
  attachments 181–2
  housekeeping 180–1
  security and control 180
  timing, style, content 181
Bigfoot 164
block capitals 148
boot sector viruses 78
breach of confidence 98, 102–3

confidential information 102–3
duty of confidence 102
information protection 103
liability 103
British Airways (BA) 134
British Standards Institute (BSI) 51–2, 54
Code of Practice 51–2, 54
British Telecom (BT) 3
browser, definition 187
Bubbleboy virus 79
bulletin board, definition 187–8
Business & Accounting Software
Developers Association (BASDA) 10
business case 4–5
business e-mail policy 115–37
alternative approaches to risk 117–18
characteristics 125–6
communication 128–31
content 118, 124–5
disclaimers and confidentiality 135
education and training 133–6
example statements 171–82
existing policies and procedures 131–3
firewalls and filters 135
insurance policies 136
internal and external mail 120
maximizing benefits 120–1
necessity 116–21
organization involvement 126
policy creation 121–4
related material 133
risks 118–19
Business Names Act 1985 110–11
business processes 9–11
business risk 11–15

Centre for Dispute Resolution (CEDR)
111

certificate revocation lists (CRL) 169
certificates 168
definition 187
Certification Authorities (CAs) 84, 168
chain mail 11, 19
changing messages 11
chat rooms 39
definition 39, 188
checklist 161–2
Christmas tree virus 15
Civil Procedures Rules 110
click on notices 130
client, definition 188
close and signature 146–7
closer look at e-mail 25–48
future 43–8
key characteristics 26–34
related topics 34–43
communications revolution 2–6
affordability 3
e-mail business case 4–5
Internet access 3–4
role of e–mail 5–6
science fiction to reality 2
Companies Act 1985 110
Companies Act 1989 110
company
effect of size 121
information 35–7
roles 59
stationery 58, 110–11
web site see web site
compression algorithms 42
definition 188
computer misuse 98, 108
Computer Misuse Act 1990 98, 108–9
Computer Weekly 117
confidentiality 74
keeping things secret 74–5

content 19
    checker 81
    legislation 47
contract 19
    inadvertent formation 98
copies 4, 31
Copyright, Designs and Patents Act 1988
        105
copyright infringement 98, 105
copyright material 19
cost 28–9
creating good messages 139–62
    addressing messages 142–4
    attachments 148–52
    good messages 140–1
    other features 155–8
    protecting messages 155
    purpose 141–2
    rules 158–62
    structure 145–8
    writing clearly 153–4
cyberliability 94

dangers *see* e-mail as business risk
Data Encryption Algorithm (DEA) 82
Data Encryption Standard (DES) 82–3,
        167
    definition 83
data protection 98, 107–8
Data Protection Act 1998 107–8
Data Protection Commissioner 107
date and time 157–8
declaration 129
decompression (algorithm) software,
        definition 188
defamation 98–101
    libel 99–101
Defamation Act 1996 100–1

Deleted mail 34
    management 68
deleting messages 12, 56–7
    management 57
diary management 40
digital signature 30, 169–70
    authentication 77
    definition 188, 192
    integrity 76
    legislation 47
    and certificates 83–4
directory services 164–5
disclaimers and confidentiality notices
        135, 175, 183–8
    bank 184
    global technology advisory firm 184
    healthcare company 185
    law firm 183
    security firm 185
    utility company 183
disclosure in legal proceedings 98, 109
disk storage space 50–1
Distribution Lists 26, 61
    definition 188
document management 39
domain name 58–9
    definition 188
download, definition 188
dragging and dropping files 27

e-commerce 42–3
E-Mail Address Book 164
e-mail in business 6–11
    business processes 9–11
    external communications 8–9
    internal communications 6–8
    working practices 9
e-mail as business risk

hidden dangers 11–13
reality vs hype 1–15
e-mail and the law 93–114
    actions 96
    answers to questions worth asking
        112–13
    company stationery 110–11
    effective service 110
    general aspects 94–6
    key aspects of the law 98–109
    questions worth asking 96–7
    taking legal action 111
    which law applies 95
e-mail in practice 20–3
    Western Provident Association (WPA)
        20–3
e-mail working for you 15–20
    flexibility and control balance 18
    personal use of business e–mail
        16–17
    policies and guidelines for staff
        17–18
    rules of good usage 15–16
    seven deadly sins 18–20
ease of use 26–7
eBIS (electronic Business Interchange
    Standard) 10
education and training 130, 133–6
electronic Business Interchange Standard
    (eBIS) 10
Electronic Data Interchange (EDI),
    definition 189
electronic original, legislation 48
electronic postcards 30
emoticon, definition 189
encryption 30, 82–5, 88
    asymmetric 83, 187
    definition 189
    legislation 48

RSA 192
standards 82–3
storage 54
symmetric 82–3
trusted third party archiving 58
Engel, David 93–114
Enigma 86
etiquette see netiquette
executable, definition 189
external communications 8–9, 117
Extranets 37
    definition 189

file types 149–50
filters 81, 135
    client 63
    definition 62, 189
    pornography 62
    server-level 63
filters and auto-management facilities
        62–4
    auto-management facilities 63–4
    filters 62–3
firewalls 29, 81, 135
    definition 189
flames 19
    definition 189
flexibility and control balance 18
flooding 81
folders 34, 53–4
    definition 189
forms 10
forward system 5
Four 11 164
France, cryptography 89
Freeserve 40
frequently asked questions (FAQs) 35
future 43–8

legislation 47–8
message management 46–7
mobile phones and PDAs 44–5
security 47
unified messaging 45–6

glossary 187–94
greeting, close and signature 158
greeting/salutation 145
Groupware and Workflow 39–49
    Groupware definition 39, 189
    Workflow, definition 39, 194

heated messages 19
helpdesk 35, 59
Hertfordshire County Council 29
Hester, Paul 13
hierarchies 6–7
hostmaster 59
housekeeping 175–6, 180–1
Howes, Peter 68
hyperlink, definition 190
hypertext, definition 190
Hypertext Mark-up Language (HTML) 32, 148
    definition 190
    virus 79

identity 20
IMAP4 66
    definition 190
in-tray management 57–8
inadvertent formation 108
Inbox 34
    management 57–8, 68
info 59

information overflow 7–8
information protection 73
insurance policies 136
Integralis Network Systems 74, 87
integrity 20, 74–6
    content 76
    delivery 75–6
internal communications 6–8
    hierarchies to networks 6–7
    information overflow 7–8
internal and external mail 120
international e-mail 154
    date format 154
    monetary unit 154
Internet 34–7
    access 3–4
    definition 190
    security 72
    uses 3–4
    and World Wide Web 34–5
Internet service provider (ISP) 19
    cost 28
    definition 190
    domain name 58–9
Intranets and Extranets 37
    definition 37, 190
introduction 1–24
    communications revolution 2–6
    e-mail as a business risk 11–15
    e-mail in practice 20–3
    effect of e-mail in business 6–11
    making e-mail work for you 15–20
InTuition 14, 29, 1120
ISP see Internet service provider (ISP)
IT Network Journal 78

Japan, Internet 4
junk mail 14, 19

key characteristics 26–34
  accessibility 30–1
  attachments 32–4
  cost 28–9
  ease of use 26–7
  folders 34
  security 30
  speed 27
KPMG Management Consulting 8, 51

law *see* legislation
layout 147
Leez Priory 35
legal action 111
  see also e-mail and the law
legislation 12, 47–8
  see also e-mail and the law
libel 99–101, 119
Lotus Domino 29
low cost 4
Lycos 165

Macro viruses 78–9
mail management 49–70
  addresses, address lists, distribution lists
    58–61
  aims 50–1
  attachments 61–2
  filters and auto-management facilities
    62–4
  good practice 51–3
  managing messages 53–8
  mobile workforce 66
  rules of good e-mail management 68–9
  spam 64–6
  working off-line 67–8
  see also message management

mail standards 176–8
Mailing list 38, 60
  active 38
  definition 38, 190
  moderated 38
  passive 38
  unmoderated 38
management practice 51–3
  role of service provider 52–3
  standards 52
managing mail *see* mail management
marketing 59
Marketing & Communication Agency
    (MCA) 134
Melissa virus 11
Message Digest Three (MD3) 170
message management 46–7, 53–8,
    119
  deleting messages 56–7
  folders 53–4
  in-tray management 57–8
  sent messages 58
  storing, backing up, archiving,
    retrieving messages 54–6
  see also creating good messages
message structure 145–8
  close and signature 146–7
  greeting/salutation 145
  layout 147
  text format 147–8
Microsoft 13
  Excel 90, 179
  Exchange 29, 151
  Internet Explorer 34
  Outlook 165
  Word 178
Microsoft Outlook 2000 30, 91
  Address book 60
  encryption facilities 84

Inbox 58
Inbox Assistant 58, 63
Out of Office Assistant 63–4
Microsoft Word, password protection
86
MIME, definition 190
misstatement 98, 106–7
mobile phones and PDAs 44–5
mobile workforce 66
modem, definition 191
Moore, Gordon 3
Moore's law 3

National Computer Centre (NCC) 78
National Westminster Bank 13
NetFind 165
netiquette 31
Netscape 165
    Communicator 91, 165
    Navigator 35
Network Associates 84
Newsgroups 38
    definition 38, 191
    off-line working 67
Nokia 43
Norwich Union, Western Provident
    Association (WPA) 13, 94

obscene material 98
    publication 105–6
off-line working 67–8
    definition 191
Ogley, Bill 29
on-line, definition 191
Open Relay Behaviour–modification
    System (ORBS) 65–6
operating system, definition 191

Outbox 34
Ovum 45

password 20, 69
    control 80
Personal Digital Assistants (PDAs)
    44
    definition 191
personal use of business e-mail 16–17,
    173–4
PGP (Pretty Good Privacy) 84
    definition 191
plain text 32
    definition 191
Point-of-Presence, definition 191–2
policies and guidelines for staff
    17–18
    see also business e-mail policy
policy creation 121–4
POP3, definition 192
pornography, filter 62
Portable Data File (PDF) 152
    definition 191
postmaster 59
priority 155
privacy 20, 98
program viruses 78
protection 155, 178–80
    message 155
    see also security
protocol 31
    definition 192
Public Key Infrastructure (PKI) 83, 85, 92,
    166–70
    certificate revocation lists 169
    certificates and certificate authorities
    168
    definition 191

digital signatures 169–70
public and private key pairs 166–8
Public Order Act 1986 105
purpose, timing and content 159

QA Research 94

Race Relations Act 1976 104–5
racial harassment 98, 104–5, 119
racist material 19
Rainier Limited 35–6
Reply All button 26–7
Reply button 26
retrieving 54–6
definition 54
risk 117–19, 177
operational 73
reputational 73
see also e-mail as business risk;
security
role of e-mail 5–6
ways of using e-mail in business 6
role of service provider 52–3
RSA, definition 192
RTF, definition 192
rules of good e-mail messages
158–62
addressing and subject lines 158
attachments 160–1
checklist 161–2
greeting, close and signature 158
purpose, timing and content 159
security 160
style and format 159–60
rules of good management 68–9
rules of good usage 15–16
Russia, cryptography 89

S-MIME, definition 192
sales 59
screensaver 80
security 19, 30, 47, 71–92, 160
attachments 85
categorizing information 73
elements 74–82
encryption 82–5
operational considerations 86–8
practice 89–91
product choice 88–9
unauthorized access 80–1
security case studies 89–91
distributed group 90–1
financial institution 91
small business 90
security and control 180
self-extracting file, definition 192
Sent mail 34
management 68
sent messages 58–9
see also creating good messages
server, definition 192
server software 29
service provider 19
role 52–3
seven deadly sins 18–20
content 19
contract 19
identity 20
integrity 20
privacy 20
security 19
viruses 19
Sex Discrimination Act 1975 104
sexist material 19, 119
sexual harassment 98, 104
SLA, definition 192
smileys 156–7

SMS, definition 192
SMTP 81
   definition 193
spam 14, 29, 64–6
   company protection 65
   definition 193
   legislation 47
   management 64–6
speech recognition 40–1
   definition 193
speech synthesis 40–1
   definition 193
speed 5, 27
   creation 27–8
   delivery 28
staff policies and guidelines 17–18
Stainton, Julian 20–3, 111
standards 52, 176–8
stationery 117
storing 5, 54–6
   definition 54
storing, backing up, archiving, retrieving
      messages 54–6
   trusted third party archiving 56
Stuffit 151
style and format 159–60
subject line 143–4
   concise subject line 144
   meaningful subject line 143
   relevant subject line 144
Switchboard 164
symbols, characters and abbreviations 157
symmetric encryption 193
system administrator, definition 193
system attacks 74
system monitoring 174

TCP/IP, definition 193

text editor, definition 193
text format 80, 147–8
text-to-speech (TTS) 40–1
Theodore Goddard 111
   Cyberliability Service 94
   Western Provident Association (WPA)
      94
three-letter acronym (TLA) 82
timing, style, content 181
trusted third party
   archiving 56
   Certification Authorities (CAs) 84

UK
   Department of Trade and Industry 4–5
   Internet 4
Unified Messaging 45–6
   definition 45, 193
Uniform Resource Locator (URL) 36–7
   definition 193
unsolicited bulk e-mail 14, 29, 64
upload, definition 193
US National Board of Standards, DES 83
USA, encryption 89
usage, rules 15–16
UserId 20, 80

video-mail 42, 130–1
virus checkers 88
viruses 11, 14–15, 19, 77–80, 119
   anti-virus software 19, 79
   attachments 33
   Bubbleboy 79
   Christmas tree 15
   definition 193
   legislation 47
   macro viruses 78–9, 109

Melissa 11
program viruses 78–9
protection against infection 79–80
security 74
threat 77–9
transmission 98, 109
virus checkers 29, 69, 81–2
Visual Basic Script 78
volume of messages 8

Waddington, Stephen 37
web site 35–7
web-based e-mail 194
webmaster 59
Western Provident Association (WPA) 13,
20–3, 94, 111, 155
WhoWhere 164
Winzip 151
Wireless Application Protocol (WAP)
45
    definition 193
Workflow *see* Groupware and Workflow
working practices 9
    definition 194
World E-Mail Directory 164
World Wide Web (WWW) 29, 34–7
    definition 194
writing clearly 153–4

Yahoo! 165

KING ALFRED'S COLLEGE
LIBRARY